IQBAL
HIS LIFE
AND
OUR TIMES

Some Other Books by the Author

Iqbal: an Illustrated Biography
The Republic of Rumi: a Novel of Reality
The Beast and the Lion
Shakespeare According to Iqbal
2017: the Battle for Marghdeen

Edited

Stray Reflections: the Private Notebook of Iqbal
Javidnama (abridged)

IQBAL

HIS LIFE
AND
OUR TIMES

Khurram Ali Shafique

Iqbal: His Life and Our Times
http://www.marghdeen.com

UK/US edition
ISBN: 978-0-9571416-6-7

General edition published by
ECO Cultural Institute
http://www.ecieco.org
and
Iqbal Academy Pakistan
http://www.iap.gov.pk

UK/US edition simultaneously published by
Libredux Publishing, Nottingham
http://www.libredux.com

Fain would I see such glad turmoil,
With a free people stand on a free soil.
To such a moment past me fleeing,
Tarry, I'd cry, thou art so fair!
                    Johann Wolfgang von Goethe (1749-1832)

Given character and healthy imagination, it is possible to reconstruct this world of sin and misery into a veritable paradise.

Dr. Sir Muhammad Iqbal (1877-1938)

Contents

Introduction

Dr. Sir Muhammad Iqbal (1877-1938) is the only poet and thinker in the history of world literature who has been credited with the birth of a new nation and a new state. It is therefore very befitting that a handbook about his life and thought should be brought out by an organization comprising ten member states. The Economic Cooperation Organization's Cultural Institute (ECI) is pleased to bring out this publication jointly with Iqbal Academy Pakistan.

In addition to his unique status in Pakistan, Iqbal also happens to be either a national poet or a household inspiration in several other countries including Iran, Tajikistan, Kazakhstan, Kyrgyzstan, Turkmenistan, Uzbekistan and India. In Turkey, his symbolic grave stands in the compound of the mausoleum of Maulana Jalaluddin Rumi. In the universities of Heidelberg and Cambridge, there are chairs or fellowships in his name. Roads, buildings and monuments have been named after him in other countries too, including Mauritius.

Iqbal: His Life and Our Times fulfils the need for a simple and reliable introduction to the life and work of this unmatched genius, highlighting the practical relevance of his ideas for those who wish to consider them for implementation. The author, Khurram Ali Shafique, is well known in the field of Iqbal Studies. The awards that he has received for his previous publications include the coveted Presidential Iqbal Award.

The present volume includes many findings that are the outcome of the author's original research. Of special interest to general readers as well as to experts would be the evidence, presented here for the first time, which establishes a historical connection between the political ideas of Iqbal, the American thinker Mary Parker Follett and the Bengali visionary C. R. Das. We are hoping that this volume will offer much by way of looking at present times from new avenues:

- it is shown here that the views expressed by Iqbal in his poetry and prose formed a coherent system of thought, and the same was implemented by him through political and social action;[1]
- this system of thought and its underlying principles are being presented here, perhaps for the first time;
- it is also being shown that in spite of its inner coherence, the system of Iqbal's thought kept pace with the evolution of the collective life of his community;
- this evolution can be studied by dividing the intellectual life of the poet-philosopher into three stages: inquiry, discovery and transcendence; the duration of each stage has been established here on the basis of biographical and textual evidence, and the book has been divided into three chapters accordingly;
- each of these three stages started in his mental life when his community adopted a new goal collectively; the goals, their relevance to the world and humanity, their implications for Iqbal, and his contribution towards achieving them are issues that are being discussed here in a fresh light; and this may turn out to be one of the most significant contributions that this book will make to the subject.

---

[1] This is to dispel a myth that has been preventing a deeper understanding of Iqbal's thought until now, i.e. the false but widely perpetuated assumption that the ideas presented by Iqbal were either inconsistent with each other or they underwent so many changes during his life that they cannot be considered for implementation in any other time.

If the nations of the world desire to come closer in their hearts and minds, they cannot afford to ignore learning about the ideas, emotions and visions of one another. The Economic Cooperation Organization's Cultural Institute (ECI), formed through a charter at the third summit meeting of the countries of ECO[1] held at Islamabad in 1995, aims at fostering understanding and the preservation of the rich cultural heritage of its members through common projects in the fields of media, literature, art, philosophy, sport and education.

The present volume is being offered in line with this vision, and with the conviction that it is important for everybody to be informed about the ideas of Iqbal, since they may be counted among those cultural forces that have gone into shaping a significant part of our world.

This conviction is shared by Iqbal Academy Pakistan, a statutory body of the Government of Pakistan, originally established through an act of parliament in 1951 and reinforced through an ordinance in 1962. The aims and objectives of the Academy are to promote and disseminate the study and understanding of the works and teachings of Iqbal. The Academy has been translating its objectives into action through a number of measures including publication programmes, IT projects, outreach activities, the Iqbal Award Programme, websites, research and compilation, audio-video, multimedia, archive projects as well as exhibitions, conferences, seminars, projection abroad, research guidance, academic assistance, donations and library services.

---

[1] The Economic Cooperation Organization (ECO) is an intergovernmental regional organization established in 1985 by Iran, Pakistan and Turkey for the purpose of promoting sustainable economic, technical and cultural cooperation among the member states, which now include also Afghanistan, Azerbaijan, Kazakhstan, Kyrgyz Republic, Tajikistan, Turkmenistan and Uzbekistan. It is the successor organization of Regional Cooperation for Development (RCD) which remained in existence from 1964 to 1979.

We hope that readers will benefit from the book that we are offering here jointly, and that this will go a long way in achieving our common objectives.

Iftikhar Husain Arif   Muhammad Suheyl Umar
President,   Director,
ECO Cultural Institute,   Iqbal Academy Pakistan,
Tehran   Lahore

Prologue
Marghdeen

The city of Marghdeen is a magnificent place with tall buildings. Its people are beautiful, selfless and simple; they speak a language that sounds melodious to the ears. They are not after material goods; rather they are the guardians of knowledge and derive wealth from their sound judgement. The sole purpose of knowledge and skill in that world is to help improve life. Currency is unknown, and temperaments are not governed by machines that blacken the sky with their smoke. Farmers are hardworking and contented – there are no landlords to plunder their harvest, and the tillers of the land enjoy the entire fruit of their labour. Learning and wisdom do not flourish on deceit and hence there is neither army, nor law keepers are needed, because there is no crime in Marghdeen. The marketplace is free from lies and the heartrending cries of the beggars.

This is a summary of how Dr. Sir Muhammad Iqbal described his ideal world in the fifth book of his poetry. It is neither the welfare state of the capitalist nor the godless society of the communist. It is something else, and something beyond. Yet, it cannot be discarded as utopia. Millions have pledged their souls to the achievement of this dream. More are likely to join the ranks, and they are not dissidents and revolutionaries. They are nations and states.

Not surprisingly, the number of books written about Iqbal runs into thousands, and Iqbal Academy Pakistan boasts of bringing out publications in more than twenty languages, the bulk of which includes some highly acclaimed biographies as well. Still, the present volume is different. It is the first biography of Iqbal that aims at nothing more – but nothing less – than tracing the development of the idea of Marghdeen in his mind, and telling the story for the benefit of those who might be interested in realizing this ideal in the present times.

The beginning

Like another well-known story, the story of Marghdeen also begins with a dream. Sheikh Nur Muhammad, the father of Iqbal, had a dream in which he saw a multi-coloured bird flying in the air, while a crowd stood admiring it. Everyone in the crowd was wishing to have that bird, but it chose to descend on him. When he woke up, he interpreted the dream to mean that he was going to be blessed with a son who would grow up to earn fame. The child was aptly named Iqbal – literally meaning 'fortune' or 'glory' – when he was born in Sialkot on November 9, 1877.[1]

Family

His parents had been married in 1857. Nur came from a family of Kashmiri immigrants to Sialkot, descending from the Sapru clan of the Brahmin caste, who had converted to Islam in the fourteenth century AD. He was born sometime around 1827 (the exact year of birth is not known). He was better known by his

---

[1] See 'Chronology' for alternative dates of birth.

nickname 'Nathoo' but youngsters in the family referred to him by the honorific 'Mian Ji', especially in his later days. He was a mild-tempered man who made his living by selling Kashmiri shawls, drawstrings and caps from a shop in the front room of his house (and some of these items were prepared by women in the family). Still, his temperament was not suited to business, and he eventually handed over the shop to a son-in-law in the 1890s. By nature, he was an ascetic whose lack of formal education did not prevent him from mastering complex themes of Divine Love from discussions held in the gatherings of local Sufi masters. Out of affection, one of his friends called him *un parh falsafi* (untutored philosopher).[1]

Imam Bibi, Iqbal's mother, also came from a family of Kashmiri immigrants. She was a down to earth woman with a firm grip on the material aspects of life. Her views about religion were quite straightforward, in stark contrast to the mysticism of her husband.[2] The long years of domestic happiness that this odd couple is reported to have enjoyed could be taken as evidence of some extraordinary sensitivity in both of them.

Sheikh Muhammad Iqbal, their fourth child to survive infancy, was preceded by a brother, Sheikh Ata Muhammad (c.1859-1940), and two sisters, Fatima and Talay. He was followed by two more sisters, Karim and Zainab.[3]

Early years

Iqbal was around two when his right eye became dysfunctional, after leeches were applied as a traditional remedy for some illness. He grew up with this handicap ('I do not remember ever

---

[1] Shafique (Urdu; 2009), pp.12, 16, 18, 27, 30-31, 38-39, 82
[2] Shafique (Urdu; 2009), p.18-19
[3] Shafique (Urdu; 2009), pp.22, 27, 28, 38, 43.

seeing anything with my right eye,' he is reported to have said later).[1] This may explain his preference in the later years for being photographed in profile, keeping his right eye away from the camera. More seriously, he was disqualified for civil service on medical grounds in his early twenties.[2]

The house was teeming with relatives when he was growing up. He was a very social child, who also excelled in studies.[3] Initially, those studies comprised almost entirely of recognizing the Arabic alphabet and learning sections of the Quran by heart, because his education started in a mosque school.[4]

This was in keeping with the pledge which Sheikh Nur Muhammad had made after seeing that dream some time before the birth of Iqbal. He had decided to dedicate his son to the 'service of Islam'.

The milieu

Since Islam and Muslim – faith and believer – were interchangeable in the parlance of those days, to serve Islam was practically to serve the Muslim community, and this is what Iqbal grew up to do.

Five degrees of love

Serving his own community did not mean hostility towards, or even rivalry with, other communities and religions.

---

[1] Hameed Ahmad Khan (1974) *Iqbal ki Shaksiyat aur Shaeri* [Iqbal's Personality and Poetry], p.50 cited in Shafique (Urdu; 2009), p.38
[2] Abdullah Qureshi (Urdu; 1988, Ed.), *Tazkar-e-Iqbal* [Memoirs of Iqbal], p.50 cited in Shafique (Urdu; 2009), p.201-202
[3] Khalid Nazeer Sufi (1971), *Iqbal Darun-i-Khana* [Iqbal In His Home], p.75 cited in Shafique (Urdu; 2009), p.43-44
[4] Shafique (Urdu; 2009), p.42

Syed Ahmad Khan (knighted in 1888) and his Bengali associate Nawab Abdul Latif of Calcutta, who had launched a movement of social reform in India soon after its takeover by the British in 1857, had based their worldview on the Sufi paradigm of love. Personal relationships, community, humanity, Nature and the universe were seen as gradually rising notes of a single emotion, i.e. love.[1] By adhering to the norms of love in personal relationships, one could rise to a vision of love for his or her group, and by fulfilling one's obligations towards the group – i.e. community, society or nation – one could rise to the still higher callings of love for humanity, Nature and universe.

This was what the more genuine schools of Sufism had practised in their monasteries, and preached to the masses outside, for more than a thousand years. Syed was probably the first reformer to make this indigenous wisdom the basis of social activism by first reinterpreting history in the light of this idea, and then by using that history for seeking new ideals in literature, new forms of organization in politics, new insights into religion and science, and new methods of education.

The thought of Syed and his associates, apart from shaping the society in which Iqbal was growing up, also provided a foothold outside the worldviews of those Western thinkers whose ideas were shaping the world at that time: Hegel, Darwin, Karl Marx, Nietzsche, Renan, William James, and so on. The question that could be seen as a common issue for all these thinkers, in spite of the vast differences between them, was: what is the relationship between the individual, society and God? Syed and his associates were answering the same question in the same time as their more celebrated contemporaries. Yet, while the Western thinkers based their worldviews either on reason and intellect, or on instinct and brute force, Syed and his

---

[1] Sheikh Muhammad Ismail Panipati, Ed. (1972-3/2009), pp.41, 48-49

friends based theirs on love, and the power of love to transform things. Iqbal inherited it, and the story of his mind turns out to be the history of the development of a lesser-known school of modern thought that has been running parallel to the better-known schools, addressing the same issues as them and intersecting their paths at times, but which has still maintained its distinct identity.[1]

The soul of all human beings

If love was to be the basis of a worldview, the object of love had to be defined clearly. In an allegory published in 1873, Syed described 'the soul of all human beings' as 'the good deed that lasts forever', and personified it as a celestial bride of outstanding beauty. The way of winning her heart was by serving 'the entire humankind, especially one's own community.'[2]

Community or nation, in British India in 1873, could mean in the narrower sense the caste, clan, ethnicity or religious sect. In its noblest sense, it could mean the religion to which one belonged, regardless of one's particular sect. Syed advocated this broader conception of community – or rather the *broadest* conception, since a composite Indian nation comprising of all religions was not in existence, nor had it even been dreamed of.[3]

For the Indian Muslims, then, the starting point for wooing the Celestial Bride – 'the soul of all human beings' – was to serve the Indian Muslim community. They did that – especially the youth, as they became enchanted by this beautiful heroine,

---

[1] While most of those other schools have culminated on a pessimist outlook in our times, the outcome of the school represented by Iqbal is Marghdeen.

[2] Panipati, Ed. (1990), p.261

[3] This is often missed by those who suggest that Sir Syed had proposed 'Two-Nation Theory'. The existence of Muslims and Hindus as two separate nations was a well-understood fact at that time, and did not require any 'theory'.

who could at once be identified with humanity as well as one's own community. The college founded by Syed at Aligarh in 1877 (the year when Iqbal was born), and the modern education represented by it, were not ends in themselves. They were means for arriving at the doorsteps of 'the soul of all human beings' – the Celestial Bride.[1]

This was a type of nationalism essentially compatible with the ideal principles of the contemporary Western civilization (freedom, equality and solidarity), but also capable of going beyond that civilization, which had failed to make its idealism a living factor in its life.[2]

Syed Mir Hasan

This worldview, which was later named the Aligarh Movement, was most prominently represented in Sialkot by Maulvi Syed Mir Hasan, a vernacular Muslim teacher in the local Scotch Mission School. He was the same friend who had given Sheikh Nur Muhammad the nickname, 'the untutored philosopher'. He took notice of Iqbal as an exceptionally bright child when Iqbal was a little over four.[3] He persuaded Nur to send the boy to Scotch Mission School for receiving modern education.

Thus Hasan became Iqbal's teacher in the earlier grades. Informally, he remained his mentor even afterwards.[4] 'I'm the book that he wrote,' Iqbal is reported to have said about him.[5]

---

[1] For details of this perspective, see Gilani Kamran (Urdu; 1977).

[2] 'The idealism of Europe never became a living factor in her life...' (see Iqbal [1930/1934], p.170). See also *Systems* (2012) by Saleena Karim for a further development of this argument to the effect that neither capitalism nor socialism succeeded in combining all three ideals: the former sacrificed equality for the sake of freedom while the latter went the other way around.

[3] For his detailed biography, see Dr. Sultan Mahmood Husain (Urdu; 1981). Relevant information is offered in Shafique (Urdu; 2009), pp.22-25, 27, 29-30.

[4] Shafique (Urdu; 2009), pp.44-46

[5] Shafique (Urdu; 2012), p.776

The guiding principle

This remark and other reports about Iqbal's devotion to his mentor serve as reminders of where he was coming from.

Mohammedan Educational Conference

He was nine years old when his mentor went away on one of his visits to Aligarh. This time, it was for participating in a meeting of sixty-seven representatives of the Indian Muslim community from across the region on December 27, 1886. Unanimously, they adopted a resolution moved by Syed for creating an organization that could hold annual meetings in a different city each year, so that decisions about 'the education and progress' of the community could be taken through mutual consultation, and thus the Indian Muslims may become a nation in reality as they were in name.[1] The organization was named Mohammedan Educational Congress (later changed to 'Conference').

Instinctively, the founders of the MEC had shown themselves to be in sync with the spirit of their times. The territorial nationalism, still popular with the conservative politicians in Europe, was losing favour with a large number of visionaries around the world. The work that had been carried out in the previous decades by the giants of science and philosophy (such as those listed earlier) had provided bases for such diverse ideologies as socialism, fascism, Nazism, theosophy, anarchism, and many more. The 1880s were the times when organized efforts were initiated throughout the world for replacing the existing foundations of societies with one or the other of these ideologies. Even in British India, a group of the educated elite had founded the Indian National Congress in 1885 (just a year

---

[1] Shafique (Urdu; 2009), p.51

before MEC) for reorganizing the Indian society on the basis of geographical unity, an idea derived from Western education (according to one of its later presidents, Muhammad Ali Jauhar).

Against this background, the founding of the MEC was consistent with the current of the times, but unlike others, the founders of the MEC did not seek to replace the existing foundations of society with a new ideology. Instead, they resolved to achieve nationhood on the basis of beliefs that were already shared by all members of the community. Yet, their conception of nationhood was consistent with the unity of humankind.

The worldview that was being developed by Syed and his community in the preceding decades now became associated with a tangible goal.

Seek consensus

At the same time, the founding of the MEC also provided the guiding principle through which the worldview represented by it was to be implemented, and the collectively adopted goal to be achieved (and the principle turned out to be one that Iqbal would follow diligently throughout his life). In his foundational speech, Syed stated:

> We should meet and convey to each other our views regarding the education and progress of the nation. Whatever mistake there might be in our thinking should get corrected through the views of others, and the course of action acceptable to everybody should be adopted.[1]

---

[1] Quoted in Shafique (2012), p.29

This principle was derived from the injunction of the Quran that the believers should consult each other in all affairs of collective life.[1] After the first four caliphs, it could never become as important in the life of the Muslim community as it became now for the Indian Muslims through the annual sessions of MEC and other organizations that soon sprang up as offshoots.

This principle, with its emphasis on the collective will and contributing towards commonly adopted goals, became the defining factor of the cultural atmosphere in which Iqbal grew up.

Unfortunately, it also happens to be the one thing that most scholars writing about him after his lifetime have failed to observe.[2] While they have showed radical changes in his thought (e.g. a shift from patriotism to Muslim nationalism, or from metaphysical mysticism to a different kind of philosophy), they have usually failed to see any unchanging, unbending and unyielding proposition in his mental life. This has resulted in a failure to discover any coherent system of thought that could be derived from his writings for those who have been eager to implement his ideas in his own homeland, in other Muslim states and in the world at large.

No wonder then, that Marghdeen, the ideal world of Iqbal, seems elusive although his community has long fulfilled the condition prescribed by him for its creation. The need for a coherent account of his thought cannot be overemphasized. It can be only be discovered by observing his guiding principle.

In the jargon of his times, this principle was best described as 'the will to will the common will'.[3] To know that it was

---

[1] See, for instance, 3:159, 42:38 and 65:6.

[2] Notable exceptions include Gilani Kamran (Urdu; 1977).

[3] Mary Parker Follett (1918), p.49. This was also the germinating centre of the movement which led to the birth of Pakistan, but the country's historians have usually failed to observe this.

followed by him is the pre-requisite for understanding his mind. For example, when he addressed the nation at the peak of his career, and even as he observed that Islam was standing a trial greater than ever before, he still conceded that it was 'open to a people to modify, reinterpret or reject the foundational principles of their social structure'.[1] The proposition that he made on this occasion appeared to him to be 'the final destiny', and yet he said, 'I propose, not to guide you in your decisions, but to attempt the humbler task of bringing clearly to your consciousness the main principle...'[2] His lectures, the *Reconstruction,* were hailed by his audience as 'the greatest, the noblest and the finest gospel that our age has to give'.[3] Yet he wrote in the preface, 'other views, and probably sounder views than those set forth in these lectures, are possible.'[4]

These are a few examples of how the guiding principle was put into practice by Iqbal. Other examples can be found in the present volume. It is hoped they will show conclusively that every transformation in the thought of Iqbal was in sync with some new goal that his community adopted at that time, and that these goals were consistent with the noblest ideals coming forth elsewhere in the world.

This is something that also distinguishes Iqbal from contemporary Western poets like W. B. Yeats and T. S. Eliot on one hand, and from subsequent Muslim thinkers like Abul Ala Maududi and Seyyed Hossein Nasr on the other (in spite of any parallels that may be drawn between their ideas). Unlike those intellectuals and reformers, Iqbal never took it upon himself to tell the community what it should do. Instead, he placed his intellectual energies at the disposal of his people.

---

[1] Shafique (2006/2007), p.136
[2] Shafique (2006/2007), pp.139, 135
[3] Iqbal (1967/1981), p.101
[4] Iqbal (1930/1934), p.v

Born to serve rather than dictate, he became the conduit through which the collective dreams of the masses were articulated into the language of the elite, rather than the other way around. This was a journey in which he and his people underwent three distinct stages of evolution, and the chapters of the present volume have been arranged accordingly.

Chapter One

Inquiry, 1887-1906

Around the same time when his mentor was helping Syed Ahmad Khan in founding the MEC, nine-year-old Iqbal was developing an early interest in music and poetry. He started purchasing small booklets of popular Punjabi ballads, singing them to women in the house as they worked at night preparing items to be sold in the shop of Sheikh Nur Muhammad.[1] Lectures about the metaphysical teachings of Ibn-ul-Arabi were also being hosted at the house around this time, and Iqbal received permission to attend them.[2]

The directive energy

The mental activity triggered in this manner went through a gradual evolution of thought in the subsequent years, but three emotions picked up at an early age stayed throughout:

a. *A desire to be buried near the tomb of the Prophet* was born early in life, as soon as his father told him about the Prophet.[3]

b. *A personal and intense response to the Quran*, manifested in a lifelong habit of reciting the Holy Book

---

[1] Khalid Nazeer Sufi (1971), *Iqbal Darun-i-Khana* [Iqbal In His Home], p.8 cited in Shafique (2009), pp.56-57
[2] Shafique (Urdu; 2009), pp.42-43;
[3] Iqbal (Persian; 1973), pp.168-169

aloud in the early hours of the morning, and taking to heart the insight given by his father: 'no understanding of the Holy Book is possible until it is actually revealed to the believer just as it was revealed to the Prophet.'[1]

c. *An unconditional respect for the public opinion of his community* was evidently the influence of his mentor Maulvi Syed Mir Hasan and the Aligarh Movement, and has already been discussed as 'the guiding principle'.

These emotions, since they never left his heart at any moment in life, can collectively be described as the directive energy that steered his movement through time and illuminated his vision.

Disappointments and diversification

The time in which he grew up was an epoch of rapid changes. As an adolescent, he witnessed his hometown Sialkot transform into an industrial hub for the manufacture of sports goods and surgical instruments. Modern education seemed to be promising instant gratification through lucrative government jobs, or successful careers in such fields as law.

Unfortunately, by the time he passed the Entrance Examination (Grade 10, later known as matriculation) on May 4, 1893, he had been forced into an arranged marriage against his choice, which took place on the same date.[2] His wife, Karim Bibi (and hence a namesake of his youngest sister), was also of Kashmiri origin but came from a much wealthier family in the neighbouring town of Gujarat. She was a few years older than him, and the two seemed to have irreconcilable differences.

---

[1] Iqbal (1930/1934), p.171; see also Shafique (Urdu; 2009), p.99
[2] Muhammad Abdullah Chughtai (1977), *Rivayat-i-Iqbal*, p.26 cited in Shafique (Urdu; 2009), p.94

They may have had very little interaction apart from producing two children during the first five years of their marriage, and becoming officially separated in the twentieth. Iqbal continued to pay her a monthly stipend for the rest of his life.[1] She survived him and died in 1947.[2] Their elder child was a girl, Meraj Bano (1896-1915). The younger one was a boy, Aftab, who was born on June 23, 1898, and became increasingly estranged to his father until all contact was severed between them in 1920. He became a barrister, and died in 1979.[3]

Iqbal passed F. A. (Grade 12) from Murray College, Sialkot, two years after his marriage.[4] The same year, he left for the nearby greater city of Lahore for higher education.[5] He did not take his wife with him (nor did he bring her when he settled there permanently a few years later).[6] In Lahore, he took admission in the prestigious Government College.[7] He passed B.A. (graduation) in early 1897, securing two medals for topping in Arabic but pursued his other subject, philosophy, for masters.[8] He passed M.A. in early 1899, in third division, but still received a medal for 'topping' as the only candidate for the subject.[9]

As a student of masters he became acquainted with the famous Orientalist Thomas Arnold, the author of the groundbreaking work, *The Preaching of Islam* (1892). Arnold had come to teach at the Government College after a stint at the M.A.O. College, Aligarh, where he had been a personal friend of Sir Syed Ahmad Khan and the emerging religious scholar,

---

[1] Ijaz Ahmad (1985), *Mazloom Iqbal* [The Oppressed Iqbal], pp.101, 104, 106 cited in Shafique (Urdu; 2010), p.480
[2] Shafique (Urdu; 2010), p.506
[3] Shafique (2006/2007), pp.23, 25
[4] Shafique (Urdu; 2009), p.108
[5] Shafique (Urdu; 2009), p.111
[6] Shafique (Urdu; 2009), p.159
[7] Shafique (Urdu; 2009), pp.112-113
[8] Shafique (Urdu; 2009), p.138-139
[9] Shafique (Urdu; 2009), p.157

historian, poet and literary critic Maulana Shibli Numani. In Lahore, Arnold developed an immediate liking for Iqbal and played an influential role in shaping his career until 1908.[1]

Among the dead who influenced Iqbal during his student days, German thinkers Hegel and Goethe led him to 'the "inside" of things'. Indian Persian poets Mirza Ghalib and Bedil taught him 'how to remain oriental in spirit and expression after having assimilated foreign ideals of poetry'.[2]

About the English Romantic poet William Wordsworth, Iqbal wrote later that he 'saved me from atheism in my student days'.[3] This 'atheism' (and a phase of 'intellectual agnosticism' lasting from 1898 to 1906 according to another report) seems to be an allusion to his interest in Idealistic Speculation and metaphysical mysticism, and his desire to discover a composite Indian nationalism (discussed later in this chapter). Wordsworth may have shown him a way out by drawing him towards a more holistic engagement with Nature.

The educationist

At the end of his studies, he must have expected special rewards as the most brilliant student of the batch. Unfortunately, he flunked the Law examination.[4] He then applied for public service but was disqualified because his right eye was dysfunctional. Hence, he was stuck with a temporary job in the Oriental College, Lahore, for the first few years of his career.[5]

---

[1] Shafique (Urdu; 2009), p.123-124, 147, 151
[2] Dr. Javid Iqbal, Ed., (1961/2006), p.53
[3] Dr. Javid Iqbal, Ed., (1961/2006), p.53
[4] Shafique (Urdu; 2009), p.154. He failed in Jurisprudence, which is incidentally the subject of his most celebrated lecture in the *Reconstruction*.
[5] Shafique (Urdu; 2009), pp.156-157

Through the efforts of his former teacher Arnold, he eventually got a permanent appointment in the more prestigious Government College, but the opportunity came in 1904, only after he had already decided to change his profession.[1] He was called to bar from London in 1908, and resigned from his job soon afterwards. Informally, he remained associated with education till the very end of his career.[2]

'The Doctrine of Absolute Unity' (1900)

His first research paper, 'The Doctrine of Absolute Unity as Expounded by Abdul Karim al-Jili', was published in the *Indian Antiquary,* Bombay, in September 1900.[3]

It was the product of the same mental attitude that was later described by him as 'intellectual agnosticism'.[1] Being obviously under the influence of Hegel at that time, he was aspiring to develop a philosophical system from the Islamic heritage of metaphysical mysticism. Taking the first practical step towards that end, he introduced a classical text, *Al Insan al-Kamil* [The Perfect Human Being], to the modern readers through this paper. The author of the classic was the mystic philosopher Abdul Karim Al-Jili (1365-1408), who was also a commentator of Ibn-ul-Arabi (the Spanish mystic whom Iqbal had learnt to admire from a very young age). Comparisons were also drawn between

---

[1] Iftikhar Ahmad Siddiqui (1987) *Urooj-i-Iqbal* [The Rise of Iqbal] cited in Shafique (Urdu; 2009), p.296
[2] He was member of the senate of Punjab University, and also offered advice to Muslim University Aligarh and Usmania University, Hyderabad (Deccan). As an office-bearer of Anjuman Himayat-i-Islam, Lahore, he looked after the educational institutions running under that organization. He was also an examiner for the universities of Punjab and Allahabad. In the 1920s, he also produced textbooks of Urdu and Persian (see Chapter 2).
[3] Now included in Iqbal (1977/1995), pp.77-96; etc.

Al-Jili and modern thinkers (mostly German, such as Hegel, but excluding Nietzsche, with whom Iqbal was not yet familiar).

This initial paper became the basis for his graduation thesis at Cambridge in 1906, which was re-submitted at Munich for PhD in 1907. By then, he had actually moved away from metaphysical mysticism but a solid grounding in this domain, along with some familiarity with Vedanta and Sanskrit classics, was forever going to provide him an edge in the other important field of his expression, i.e. his poetic art.[2]

Consensus literature

As a poet, Iqbal was seen by his contemporaries as part of what was called 'the Islamic Movement of Urdu Literature' (although it later expanded to also include English, Persian and some regional languages).[3] The writings of Sir Syed, such as the earlier mentioned story about 'the soul of all human beings', were precursors to this movement which was properly launched at Syed's request by his colleague and follower Altaf Husain Hali – poet, critic and biographer. In 1879, he published his long Urdu poem, *The Ebb and Tide of Islam,* better known as *Mussadas-i-Hali,* and revised in 1886. Six years later, he defined the poetics of the movement in *Prolegomena to Poetry* (Muqqaddama-i-Shaer-o-Shaeri).

---

[1] See the diaries of Ghulam Rasool Mehr reproduced in Alvi (1988).

[2] For instance, while summarizing the gist of Al-Jili's argument, he stated in the research paper: 'The perfect man is the pivot round which revolve all the "heavens" of existence, and the sum of the realities of material existence corresponds to his unity.' [Iqbal (1977/1995), p.91]. One can recognize here some familiar metaphors from his later poetry.

[3] See Syed Naseer Ahmad B.A. (1935)

The national mind

This literary movement can be seen as a major factor in lowering those psychological barriers that could prevent the educated minds from seeking a common will with the unschooled masses. Hence, although the task of creating a collective will was the common goal of almost every nation at that time, it was going to be fulfilled only by the Indian Muslim community.

The nations of Europe, in spite of their idealism and enlightenment, failed or gave up because inadvertently they had embraced the exactly opposite trends in literature, which had been introduced in France in the 1840s and popularized in England in the 1860s. Those trends were based on a perceived dichotomy between high and low culture. Thus they raised those psychological barriers, higher than ever before, which needed to be lowered and removed in order to create a collective will.[1]

Among the Indian Muslims, the poem of Hali, which had been written as a reaction against the 'sterility and dullness' that vernacular literature had acquired since the decline of Muslim power, ended up empowering the masses by making, for the first time, the life of ancient Muslims 'personally, directly and vividly comprehensible to the philistines.'[2] Then came the irresistibly humorous poet Akbar Allahabadi, with biting satire against those whom modern education had taught to look down on the beliefs of the masses.[3] Iqbal's contemporaries believed that the combined effect of Hali and Akbar 'prepared the national mind for the reception of a poet-philosopher'.[4] To be this poet-philosopher was the destiny of Iqbal.

---

[1] Iqbal described it later as 'the reaction against Democracy in England and France' but contended that its meaning could only be grasped by looking at 'the psychological causes of this reaction.' See Iqbal (1961/2006), p.109
[2] Khan (1922/1982), p.6
[3] Khan (1922/1982), p.6
[4] Khan (1922/1982), p.7

The young poet-philosopher

While still at school, he mastered the craft of poetry, acquired a working knowledge of the classical Indian music and received some guidance from the renowned master of amorous poetry, Nawab Mirza Khan Dagh, through correspondence. By 1893, he was contributing amorous ghazals to popular magazines, and after moving to Lahore in 1895, he started participating in poetry recitals, for which he received much acclaim from local critics.

Five precepts that he seems to have picked up from the literary movement of Hali as tools for creating a collective will through literature were:

    a. the perception that Muslim culture was an effect of the spirit of the message of the Prophet of Islam and his powerful personality;[1]

    b. the aim of 'entertaining high and low alike'[2];

    c. the purpose of finding a course of action 'agreeable to everybody';[3]

    d. the willingness to be guided by public opinion; and

    e. a universal outlook, rooted in the awareness that modern European civilization was based on ideals originally introduced by Islam;[4]

Stardom

His true fame as a poet started after he joined the philanthropic organization Anjuman Himayat-i-Islam, a few months before the publication of his research paper about Al-Jili. His first long poem, recited in the annual fundraising session of the

---

[1] This was the substance of Hali's poem; see also Iqbal (1930/1934), p.118-119.
[2] Khan (1922/1982), p.7
[3] See the section 'The Guiding Principle' in the prologue.
[4] See, for example, Iqbal (1977/1995), p.103

organization in March 1900, brought him unusual acclaim. His contributions to *Makhzan,* a new magazine launched in April next year, turned him into a household name at least in those parts of British India where Urdu was spoken and understood.

In 1904, his patriotic poem 'Our Homeland' (later renamed) – with the iconic first line, 'Saray jahan say accha Hindustan hamara' – spread like wild fire across the subcontinent. It was later stated without exaggeration:

> It is rare indeed that a young man, as yet a student, should become the idol of the people, and the first fact for you to observe is that no poet ever had such vast and sudden popularity. Not only in Punjab but all over India, so great was his influence that it crushed all competition out of existence.[1]

The hallmark of his poetry was later described as 'a very high degree of consonance between that poetry's substance and form',[2] and this was perhaps because poetry to him was not a matter of choice. It came to him naturally. Hence, the vision unfolding through his poetry was not unrelated to the inquiries carried out in his prose works at that time, the next of which was on a subject far removed from metaphysical mysticism.

Political Economy (1904)

Political Economy (Ilmul Iqtisad) was Iqbal's first published book, which came out in Urdu in 1904.[3]

He developed an interest in economics partially because he had to teach the subject in the Oriental College. The outcome

---

[1] Khan (1922/1982), p.9
[2] Mir (2006), p.56
[3] Dr. Rafiuddin Hashmi (Urdu; 1982/2010), p.296

was this handbook. As a compilation of current ideas in simple language, it became obsolete during the author's lifetime. Yet, it remains indispensible as a testimony to the evolution of his thought because he we find the first clear statement about his ideal world, which he would later call Marghdeen.

This can be traced through the connection that this handbook obviously had with a string of books which had appeared in Russian by an almost identical title, usually translated as *What Is To Be Done?* They include (a) a novel about a materialistic utopia by the Russian writer Nikolai Chernyshevsky published in 1863; (b) its refutation by Leo Tolstoy published in 1886; and (c) the manifesto of Vladimir Lenin published in 1902. The title (that Iqbal was also going to use later for one of his Persian works) was an obvious reference to the third chapter of Luke, where the crowd asks John the Baptist, 'What should we do then?' John replies, 'Anyone who has two shirts should share with the one who has none, and anyone who has food should do the same.'[1]

Tolstoy argued passionately for the eradication of poverty in his *What Must Then We Do?* His argument was echoed by Iqbal in the preface of his *Political Economy*:

A question has arisen in this age, *viz.,* is poverty an unavoidable element in the scheme of things?[2] Can it not happen that the heartrending sobbing of a suffering humanity in the back alleys of our streets be gone forever and the horrendous picture of devastating

---

[1] Bible, Luke 3: 10-11 (*New International Version*)

[2] Compare with Tolstoy (1925/1942), p.104: 'When in the ancient world the entire economical order was upheld by personal slavery, the greatest intellects did not notice it. To Plato, as well as to Xenophon, and Aristotle, and to the Romans, it seemed that it could not be otherwise, and that slavery was an unavoidable and natural result of wars, without which the existence of mankind was inconceivable'

poverty wiped out from the face of the earth?[1] Economics alone cannot answer, for the answer lies in the moral capabilities of human nature...[2]

Enhancing these 'moral capabilities of human nature', therefore, was the method through which he hoped to win his ideal world. The guidelines that the handbook offered to that end were:

- The balance between individual freedom and common good is an important concern.
- Humans aspire for wealth and property, and would probably succeed in achieving these if nihilistic ideals did not rob them of aspiration.
- An economic revolution in British India was desirable.
- Economics should not be treated as a normative science. Right and wrong must be decided on moral grounds. What is useful for a community at one time may become useless or harmful at some other time, and therefore customs should be constantly revaluated and reformed.
- Freedom is inherently relevant: 'the whip cannot provide the motivation that comes only from the desire for wealth and an intense longing for self-respect.'

'National Life' (1904)

By the summer of 1904, Iqbal had almost certainly decided to go abroad for higher studies and for acquiring a bar-at-law. His elder brother Sheikh Ata Muhammad, posted at that time in the North-Western hill station of Abbotabad, was willing to help.

---

[1] Compare with Tolstoy (1925/1942), p.5: 'In Moscow it is impossible to pass a street without meeting beggars of a peculiar kind...'
[2] Translated from Urdu by the present author.

While visiting him there, Iqbal was requested by a local literary circle to deliver a lecture. Soon afterwards, he turned the contents into an essay in Urdu, 'National Life' ('Qaumi Zindagi'), published in two instalments in *Makhzan* in October 1904 and January 1905. ·

This was a time when Indian nationalism was taking giant leaps in its evolution. For administrative reasons, the British government had announced its decision of partitioning the Hindu-majority province of Bengal into two. The Indian National Congress began agitation against the decision, giving a new impetus to the nationalist sentiment. Iqbal's essay, published on the eve of nationalist agitation, amounts to contemporary evidence about how the concept of nation – or 'qaum' – was understood at that time.[1]

In the jargon of the natives, the word 'qaum' could refer simultaneously to caste, clan, profession, race, gender, religious identity, regional identity or citizenship. This reflected the actual overlap of group identities in the indigenous society, e.g. Iqbal was a Muslim by religion, a British Indian by citizenship, a Kashmiri by caste, a Brahmin by race, and a government servant (at that time) by profession. Hence, while he primarily belonged to the Muslim nation, his 'qaum' on some occasions could also be described as Indian, Kashmiri, Brahmin or government servant. The same was true, more or less, about such words as 'biradri' ('community', but also 'fraternity'), 'muashrah' (society) and 'millat' (another word for 'nation'). Also, such words were usually interchangeable.

In the essay, Iqbal used the words 'qaum' (nation) and 'muashrah' (society) exclusively for addressing the Indian Muslim nation, or the Muslim society of India – to whom he offered practical advice on surviving in the struggle for

---

[1] It may also show that the collective goal of Indian Muslims, i.e. achieving nationhood, was in harmony with the general trends of the times.

existence. He acknowledged the relationship of his community with 'fellow-nations' residing in the country (such as Hindus), but gave no hint of the existence of any composite Indian nation.

On the contrary, he stated that a nation or society was an organism born of 'the spiritual observations acquired by a prophet through his extraordinary faculties.' Beyond this, it could seek its inner cohesion in race or ethnicity (such as the Jews), or geographical unity (such as Italy), or a universal ideal (such as Islam).

Patriotic poems

Yet, he seemed to be hoping that these different nations, such as Muslims and Hindus, could be persuaded to form a composite Indian nation. Hence, the same issue of *Makhzan* in which the first instalment of his essay was published, also carried his patriotic poem, 'Our Homeland' ('Hamara Des', in Urdu), with its iconic first line, ''Saray jahan se achha Hindustan hamara', or 'Our India is better than the whole world.'[1]

The line may have been inspired by the first two lines of German national anthem, 'Deutschland, Deutschland über alles, / Über alles in der Welt,' – (Germany, Germany, above everything, / Above everything in the world,). In any case, it became phenomenally popular, as mentioned earlier, and to this date it remains imprinted on the hearts of even those Indians who do not know Urdu.

Iqbal followed up this poem with a few more on the theme of patriotism. In some of these, he represented his Muslim community to Hindu compatriots, many of whom had started

---

[1] Iqbal (Urdu; 1973), p.83 [or Iqbal (Urdu; 1990), pp.109-110]. The title of the poem was later changed to 'Indian Anthem' (Taran-i-Hindi).

taking an extremist stance.[1] 'O Brahmin, you estranged yourself to your kin in the name of idols,' he said in the Urdu poem 'The New Temple' (1905). 'Likewise, God also taught war and aggression to the preacher of Islam.' He went on to raise a new deity made of gold, venerated by the followers of all religions (and this was wisely expunged when the poem was anthologized in 1924). 'Let's label the god "India", and to him we should pray for the fulfilment of all the desires of the heart,' he said.[2]

These desires of the heart were almost certainly related to the economic revolution he had proposed in *Political Economy* (and he was always going to maintain that the economic forces in a region affected all communities alike, and hence the economic question should be approached 'in a broad impartial non-sectarian spirit'[3]).

Thus he was contemplating the possibility of a composite Indian nation, although without taking it for granted. A 'psychological analysis' of this phase of his intellectual development may be attempted in the light of a later writing, where he stated that 'when a Muslim's mind and heart are over-powered by' the idea of territorial nationalism, he or she undergoes three further stages:

a. it occurs to him or her that humankind 'has been so sharply divided into nations that it is impossible to bring about unity among them';

b. this leads to 'the conception of the relativity of religions, i.e. the religion of a land belongs to that land alone and does not suit the temperaments of other nations';

c. this must 'inevitably lead to irreligiousness and scepticism'.[4]

---

[1] See Gilani Kamran (1977).
[2] Iqbal (Urdu; 1990), p.115. See expunged lines in Shafique (Urdu; 2010), p.14-15
[3] Iqbal (1977/1995), p.136
[4] Iqbal (1977/1995), p.312

Iqbal may have been drawn towards the idea of territorial nationalism, albeit in a different form than some others, but his emotional fabric would not let him accept that 'the religion of a land belongs to that land alone' (how could it have matched with his intense desire to be buried in the city of the Prophet)! He was going to turn back very soon – before March 1907 by the latest.

England

Iqbal boarded a French steamship from Bombay on September 7, 1905, and arrived at the Dover Beach via Marseilles on September 24. He stayed in England till June 1908 (excepting a sojourn to Germany from June to November, 1907). This was the first of his three visits to the country (the next two would happen in 1931 and 1932, in connection with the Round Table Conferences of the British Indian politicians).

He entered his name in the admission register of the Trinity College, Cambridge, on October 1, 1905. A few weeks later, on November 6, 1905, he also got enrolled with the Lincoln's Inn, London, for Bar at Law. For more than a year he was going to pursue both qualifications simultaneously, commuting regularly between Cambridge and London.

Views about British people

The Aligarh Movement had taught Iqbal to look out for the positive traits in every nation that defined its place in the overall scheme of humanity. From this point of view, three positive traits of the British defined their place in the economy of nations for Iqbal:

a. The special gift of the British was the 'sense of fact', due to which purely speculative systems of thought had never become popular among them. It was no coincidence that Sir Francis Bacon, who promoted the inductive method in modern thought, was British.[1]

b. The British made the transition from absolute monarchy to democracy with less bloodshed than most other nations, and as 'law-abiding' citizens without resorting to anarchy and reigns of terror.[2]

c. In more recent times, Britain had made democracy its great mission, boldly carrying this principle to countries that had been, 'for centuries, groaning under the most atrocious forms of despotism'.

Hopefully these permanent traits of British people would last longer than the aspects of their contemporary politics that Iqbal would come to criticize very soon: territorial nationalism and the exploitation of the weaker nations.

Cambridge

Iqbal's graduation thesis at Cambridge was an extension of his Al-Jili paper: an outline of the development of metaphysical thought in Persia, from its beginnings in Zoroastrianism to its culmination in Babism. As an advanced student, he was supposed to submit it in eighteen months, and was exempted from attending classes. Since Cambridge University did not grant PhD in those days (and only DLit), he was going to be referred to a German university, like many other candidates.

His tutor was the renowned biologist Henry Sidgewick, and supervisor for the thesis was the idealist philosopher McTaggart.

---

[1] Iqbal's preface in Urdu to the first edition of 'Secrets of the Self', reproduced in Shafique (Urdu; 2012), pp.127-130

[2] Iqbal's correspondence quoted in Shafique (Urdu; 2010), pp.75

Celebrated scholars associated with the university at that time were E. G. Browne, Bertrand Russell, Wittgenstein, George Moore, A. N. Whitehead, Sorley, R. A. Nicholson and others.

The thesis was submitted on March 7, 1907. A bachelor's degree was awarded on it on June 13. The thesis may have been deemed to be of a higher standard than required, since it was going to be resubmitted, after some revision, to the Ludwig Maxmillian University, Munich, for a doctorate.

Iqbal's worldview changed radically during this period (see the next section, 'March 1907'), and he soon started developing a new framework out of two of the arguments presented in the thesis, respectively, about (a) 'faith'; and (b) something that he would later call 'the uniformity of Muslim culture'.

Faith

The Quran defined Muslims as 'those who believe in the Unseen, establish daily prayer, and spend out of what We have given them.'[1] Following various Sufi commentators, Iqbal argued from other verses of the Quran that the 'Unseen' (*ghaib*) was in one's 'own soul'.[2]

Sir Syed had famously proposed that angels, as described in the Quran, also appeared to be faculties rather than independent entities. Iqbal kept out of such theological debates for most part of his career, but continued developing a framework in which the sources for acquiring knowledge of the 'Unseen' were: (a) Nature; (b) History; and (c) Intuition.[3] Dogma had no role to play in this worldview.[4]

---

[1] Quran 2:3
[2] Chapter V in Iqbal (1908), p.108
[3] Lecture V in Iqbal (1930/1934), p.121
[4] According to Iqbal, 'religion ... in its higher manifestations is neither dogma, nor priesthood, nor ritual.' Lecture VII in Iqbal (1930/1934), p.178.

The Uniformity of Muslim Culture

Somewhat related to the elimination of dogma from his framework was his argument that European authors (including some of his superiors at Cambridge) seemed to be under the influence of the notion that 'a fixed quantity A is the cause of or produces another fixed quantity B' in the evolution of cultures. For instance, an idea travelling from Vedic India to Muslim Persia must have been responsible for all Sufi thought that appears similar to this idea.[1]

Iqbal's rejection of this approach may have been facilitated by the fact that in his own times, European ideas were permeating into his community and, as an active participant in the process, he was fully aware of the filters used by Sir Syed and his school for monitoring this permeation. As such, he was in a good position to reject the Orientalist approach, and emphasize instead the principle that 'the full significance of a phenomenon in the intellectual evolution of a people can only be comprehended in the light of those pre-existing intellectual, political, and social conditions which alone make its existence inevitable.'[2]

On the basis of this principle, he was going to argue for 'the Uniformity of Muslim Culture' a few years later, and suggest that 'mere belief in the Islamic principle, though exceedingly important, is not sufficient. In order to participate in the life of the communal self, the individual mind must undergo a complete transformation, and this transformation is secured, externally by the institutions of Islam, and internally by that uniform culture which the intellectual energy of our forefathers has produced.'[3] (Interestingly, T. S. Eliot was going to present a similar theory

---

[1] Chapter V in Iqbal (1908), p.96-98
[2] Iqbal (1908), p.97
[3] Iqbal (1977/1995), p.125

about Christianity in the 1940s, although towards a different end).[1]

Applying this principle in his thesis, he argued that the development of the Sufi doctrine in Persia was mainly an interplay between (a) the peculiar genius of the Persian people working in their own circumstances; and (b) potentialities contained in the Quran and authenticated traditions of the Prophet that, 'owing to the thoroughly practical genius of the Arabs, could not develop and fructify in Arabia.'[2] Later, he was going to elaborate further that Persia was 'perhaps the principal factor' in the making of Muslim culture. 'Our Muslim civilisation is a product of the cross-fertilisation of the Semitic [Arab] and the Aryan [Persian] ideas,' he was going to say, 'But for Persia our culture would have been absolutely one-sided.'

This gradual movement from Idealistic Speculation towards a new framework may have been partially facilitated by the intellectual atmosphere of Cambridge but it was also remarkably in sync with those dramatic changes that had began to occur throughout the Muslim world precisely at that time.

A turning of a corner

In the summer of 1906, a popular demand for democracy in Iran was led by the religious leaders of the country and resulted in the 'Constitutional Revolution' – i.e., the adaptation of a constitution, and the election of a representative parliament. Soon, the demand for democracy escalated in other Muslim countries too, especially the Ottoman Turkey and Egypt.[3] These developments were later going to be described by Iqbal as a

---

[1] See 'The Unity of European Culture' in *Christianity and Culture* by T. S. Eliot
[2] Iqbal (1908), p.107-108
[3] For details, see Shafique (Urdu; 2010), Chapter 4; pp.51-145

posthumous effect of the nineteenth century reformer Syed Jamaluddin Afghani, whose 'spirit is still working in the world of Islam and nobody knows where it will end.'[1]

In British India, Sir Syed had proposed in 1896 a scheme for separate communal electorates, drawing upon the example of Ireland where a Catholic member chosen by a Protestant constituency could not be seen as representing the true Catholic interests.[2] This idea gave birth to the first political organization of the Indian Muslims, the All-India Muslim League, on December 30, 1906. It was formed in Dacca (now Dhaka), at the venue of the twentieth annual session of the Mohammedan Educational Conference pioneered by Sir Syed Ahmad Khan twenty years earlier.

The founder of the League, Nawab Salimullah Khan, called it 'a turning of a corner of the course' adopted twenty years earlier.[3] The first president, elected a year later, was the leader of the Shia Ismaili community, Sir Sultan Mohammad Shah, Aga Khan III. This was in spite of the fact that the majority of the Muslims in India subscribed to the Sunni sect. At least in this sense, this was unarguably the greatest show of the solidarity of Islam since the days of Umar II eleven centuries earlier.

---

[1] Iqbal (1977/1995), p.231
[2] Syed Sharifuddin Pirzada (2008), p.26
[3] Syed Sharifuddin Pirzada (2008), p.135

Chapter Two
Discovery, 1907-1926

Iqbal responded to the signs of the times, and at one point he even contemplated quitting poetry in order to serve the nation better. He was dissuaded by his teacher Thomas Arnold, who argued that his poetry was also a great service to his people.[1]

'March 1907'

The vision that dawned upon him now was later going to be described by some of his biographers as 'inspired by Sir Syed's orientations', and something that he would continue to express 'in his creative poetry and lucid prose.' To strengthen and preserve the historical impulse of Muslim nationality, he 'laid down an ideological base and a stable mode of thought.'[2]

More specifically, he came to believe that the universal nation or world-state, which the Arabs had failed to create through conquest in the earlier centuries, had become possible in modern times. This was because 'life of modern political communities finds expression, to a great extent, in common institutions, Law and Government; and the various sociological circles, so to speak, are continually expanding to touch one another.' Therefore, 'the ideal nation does already exist in germ'. Further, the ideal nation was 'not incompatible with the sovereignty of individual States,

---

[1] Iqbal (Urdu; 1973), p.15; [or Iqbal (Urdu; 1990), p.43]
[2] Dr. Hafeez Malik (2009), p.135

since its structure will be determined not by physical force, but by the spiritual force of a common ideal.'[1]

Before he could elaborate these ideas in prose, the general vision flashed on him in the form of a powerful poem, 'March 1907', which was considered by him and many of his readers as 'a mine of prophesies and warnings'.[2] It began with these lines:

> The time of unveiling has come, the Beloved will be
>   seen by all;
> That secret which was veiled by silence shall become
>   manifest.
> That cycle has gone, O cup-bearer! when they drank in
>   hiding,
> The whole world shall become a tavern, and all shall
>   drink.
> Those who wandered insane shall return to dwell in
>   cities,
> Their feet shall be naked as before, but those meadows
>   shall be new.
> The silence of Makkah has proclaimed to the expectant
>   ears, at last;
> The compact which was made with the desert-dwellers
>   shall become once more strengthened.
> The Lion which came out of the wilderness and upset
>   the Empire of Rome,
> I hear from angels that he shall awaken once more.
> O dwellers of the Western lands! God's world is not a
>   shop.
> That which you considered good coin shall prove to be
>   of low value.
> Your civilization will commit suicide with its own
>   dagger;
> A nest built on a slender bough cannot last.[3]

---

[1] Iqbal (1977/1995), p.141
[2] Khan (1922/1982), p.12
[3] Iqbal (Urdu;1973a), pp.140-141. Translated by Umrao Singh in Khan (1922), p.11

Muslim nationalism

The poem was subsequently interpreted in many ways (and some of those will be discussed later in this book), but it was a bold affirmation of a political phenomenon that was becoming increasingly more manifest in the Muslim world at that time, and which Iqbal was going to call 'Muslim nationalism'.

The cornerstone of this nationalism was the belief that democracy in Muslim countries was inevitably going to lead to a new concept of 'nation' comprising of Muslims and non-Muslims as equal citizens and commonly referring to the Quran as the ultimate constitution of the state.[1]

Nationality with such a nation would be pure idea and have no geographical basis, except that the holy town of Makkah fulfilled the demand for a material centre of nationality.[2] On the other hand, European imperialism seemed to have dug its own grave, because anybody who was 'a believer in the absoluteness of races' was 'sure to be defeated by the spirit of modern times which is wholly in keeping with the spirit of Islam.'[3]

The eight-year old 'mental agnosticism' of Iqbal came to end. He was now ready to proclaim (as he did a year later):

> The law of Islam does not recognize the apparently natural differences of race, nor the historical differences of nationality. The political ideal of Islam consists in the creation of a people born of a free fusion of all races and nationalities. Nationality with Islam is not the highest limit of political development; for the general principles of the law of Islam rest on human nature, not on the peculiarities of a particular people. The inner cohesion of such a nation would

---

[1] For a detailed discussion, see Fateh Muhammad Malik (2013), pp.38-45
[2] Iqbal (1977/1995), p.114
[3] Iqbal (1977/1995), p.237

consist not in ethnic or geographic unity, nor in the unity of language or social tradition, but in the unity of the religious and political ideal; or, in the psychological fact of 'like-mindedness' as St. Paul would say. The membership of this nation, consequently, would not be determined by birth, marriage, domicile, or naturalization. It would be determined by a public declaration of 'like-mindedness' and would terminate when the individual has ceased to be like-minded with others. The ideal territory of such a nation would be the whole earth.'[1]

Atiya Fyzee

At the time of writing this prophetic poem, he had already his graduation thesis and was revising it for re-submission for PhD at Munich later that year. This is when he met the liberal aristocrat from Bombay, Atiya Fyzee, on April 1, during one of his visits to London where he had been coming regularly for attending the dinners at Lincoln's Inn.

Ms. Fyzee possessed a keen interest in Indian classical music and Persian poetry. For this, she had earned admiration of the family friend Maulana Shibli Numani, who was writing amorous ghazals for her even as she sailed to Europe in 1906 and met Iqbal the next year.[2]

Her account of her first meeting with Iqbal offers a hint of playfulness, but it seems that the flippancy soon gave way to mutual respect and matured into a lasting friendship. She may also have been the friend who asked Iqbal to write something in

---

[1] Iqbal (1977/1995), p.141
[2] See Shafique (Urdu; 2010), p.104

Persian.[1] Yet, Iqbal was evidently capable of putting her off on other occasions. 'He was much fond of himself as a man primarily – and a great scholar after. There was no getting out of it,' she wrote in an article that was published after her death. 'My first impression of "Iqbal" was that he was a "complex" – a mixture of good and evil, extremely self-contained and fond of his own opinion – a bad sign, I said to myself.'[2] Elsewhere, she assessed him as someone who regarded women as some sort of necessary evil.[3] Contrary to the wild speculations of some subsequent writers, it seems that the two were just good friends who developed some fine understanding of each other.[4] Atiya married a prominent painter in 1913.

Germany

Iqbal moved to Germany in June 1907 and stayed there till November. This visit was in connection with his doctorate.

Emma Wegenast

Emma Wegenast (August 16, 1879 – October 18, 1964) was indeed a very different case from Atiya Fyzee. Iqbal met her during his brief stay at Heidelberg in the summer of 1907, and it seems that he became emotionally attached to her. It has also been speculated that the two wanted to get married but were prevented because Emma's family did not allow her to leave Germany for settling down in British India.

---

[1] Iqbal (Urdu; 1973), p.16; [or Iqbal (Urdu; 1990), p.44]
[2] 'Iqbal – a Reflection' by Atiya Fyzee in *Dawn*, April 30, 1967, p. 15 quoted in Shafique (2006/2007), p.50
[3] See, for instance, *Illustrated Weekly of Pakistan*, April 16, 1950, p.31.
[4] Dr. Javid Iqbal (Urdu; 2008), p.218

She was the fourth child of a small business owner from Heilbronn (Germany) and was a language coach for teaching German to foreign students in Heidelberg when Iqbal met her there.[1] At 5 feet 7 inches, she was an inch taller than him.[2] She had black hair, blue eyes, and was good looking and elegant without being self-conscious. Iqbal may still have had her in mind when he offered his personal definition of beauty a little later: 'A woman of superb beauty with a complete absence of self-consciousness is probably the most charming thing on God's earth.'[3]

She acquired significance after the letters written by Iqbal to her emerged in the 1980s (her replies to Iqbal are now considered lost). Some of those letters indeed offer glimpses into the personal side of the passionate poet. For instance, sometime after returning home, he wrote to her in German: 'I've forgotten all my German, except for one word: Emma!'[4]

The period of less than six months that he spent in Germany – which included the only time in his life when he got to be with Emma – witnessed the composing of some of his most moving love poems. Emma was quite evidently the muse, but the influence of German romantic poets need not be overlooked either – Iqbal studied Goethe's *Faust* in original German in the company of Emma herself. 'Our Soul discovers itself when we come into contact with a great mind,' he wrote in a personal reflection in 1910, which was published in 1917. 'It is not until I had realized the Infinitude of Goethe's mind that I discovered the narrow breadth of my own.'[5]

---

[1] The most detailed account of Emma Wegenast and her interaction with Iqbal can be found in Durrani (Urdu; 1995).
[2] Iqbal was 5 feet 6 inches, according to his passport. See facsimile in Shafique (2006/2007), p.154
[3] Iqbal (1961/2006), p.116
[4] Letter written on September 3, 1908, cited in Shafique (Urdu; 2010), p.234
[5] Iqbal (1961/2006), p.16

Emma later served as a Red Cross nurse during the First World War, and then as a technical assistant at the University Pharmacy from 1920 to 1928. She never married.

Munich

Iqbal submitted a revised draft of his graduation thesis for a doctorate at Ludwig Maximillan University, Munich, with a letter of recommendation from Thomas Arnold. The thesis was accepted in English, but the viva voce was carried out in German (which he had mastered with Emma's help during the summer).

Since the university did not have the facility for evaluating research on Persian metaphysics, a special provision was made by treating Arabic Philology as Iqbal's principal subject, and English philology and philosophy as subsidiaries. He was awarded 1st Grade in the principal subject, and 2nd and 3rd respectively in the two subsidiaries. The doctorate was awarded Cum Laude, i.e. 'With Great Praise' in November 1907.

Back to England

Iqbal returned to England in early November 1907, and remained there till June 1908, so that he may be called to bar from the Lincoln's Inn, London. In this period, he substituted Thomas Arnold for teaching Arabic at the School of Oriental and African Studies, University of London, from November 1907 to February 1908.[1] He also delivered monthly lectures on Islam under the auspices of a Pan-Islamic Society in London,[2] and became a member of the London branch of All-India

---

[1] Shafique (Urdu; 2010), pp.172, 199
[2] Shafique (Urdu; 2010), pp.204, 205, 208

Muslim League when it was inaugurated by the renowned scholar Justice Syed Ameer Ali in May 1908.[1]

All this while, he kept dreaming about revisiting Germany on his way back home, so that he may meet Emma again, but unfortunately that was not going to happen.

Bar at Law

He was called to bar from the Lincoln's Inn, London, on July 1, 1908.[2] There is no record of how he felt on that occasion, except for the fact that his application to the Chief Court, Lahore, for being registered as a barrister was written on the same date. If this could be an indication that he felt excited about the achievement, the excitement can be fully understood. The Bar at Law must have removed from his heart the pain of having failed the law exam some nine years earlier – and, as he had admitted to Atiya Fyzee jokingly during their first meeting, he was a man for whom it was difficult to accept 'the stigma of failure.'

The Development of Metaphysics in Persia (1908)

The thesis on which he had earned a graduation from Cambridge and a doctorate from Munich was finally published by Luzac & Co., London, in June 1908 as *The Development of Metaphysics in Persia.*[3] It was dedicated to Thomas Arnold.[4] A brief note about it appeared in *Manchester Guardian* on September 15[5] and a full review in the journal *Athenaeum* on November 14.[6]

---

[1] Shafique (Urdu; 2010), p.211
[2] Shafique (Urdu; 2010), p.216
[3] Hashmi (Urdu; 1982/2010), p.306
[4] Iqbal (1908), p.v
[5] *Manchester Guardian*, September 15, p.5
[6] *Athenaeum*, Issue 4229, pp.601-602

The work was later discarded by the author on the grounds that it had become obsolete. In any case, as mentioned earlier, his creative energies had already diverted into another direction even before the book appeared in print. Yet, it has also been observed that scholarship can still benefit from the account of several thinkers and writers in it, and 'Iqbal's comparative notes about Muslim and Western thinkers still provide useful leads for future scholarship.'[1]

A new framework for understanding Islam

Sometime in early 1908, he realized that while Greek philosophy, as a great cultural force in the history of Islam, 'broadened the outlook of Muslim thinkers, it, on the whole, obscured their vision of the Quran.'[2] Under the influence of ancient Greece, early Muslim students completely missed the spirit of the Quran, 'which sees in the humble bee a recipient of Divine inspiration ...' (unlike Socrates, who had focussed on the human world alone; and his disciple Plato, who had 'despised sense-perception'). A dim perception that the spirit of the Quran was essentially anti-classical came only two centuries later. The result was a kind of intellectual revolt, the full significance of which, according to Iqbal, had not been realized until then.[3]

This awareness led him to develop a new framework for understanding Islam. It was systematically elaborated in his subsequent writings, which laid out with great clarity (a) his method; (b) purpose; (c) scope; (d) approach; and (e) some key

---

[1] Mir (2006), p.77
[2] The quotation is from Lecture I, Iqbal (1930/1934), p.3. On the origin of this idea in his mind in 1908, see Shafique (Urdu; 2010), p.209
[3] Lecture I in Iqbal (1930/1934), pp.3-4

questions.[1] These remained constant throughout his lifelong study of Islam.

Method

His position was that of a critical student, as distinguished from an expounder or a teacher.[2] Hence, he was to approach the subject 'free from all pre-suppositions' and to try 'to understand the organic structure of a religious system, just as a biologist would study a form of life or a geologist a piece of mineral.'[3]

Purpose and scope

The purpose was to comprehend the structure of a religious system and 'to estimate its ultimate worth as a civilizing agency among the forces of historical evolution.'[4] The scope was:

a. 'to discover how the various elements in a given structure fit in with one another';
b. 'how each factor functions individually'; and
c. 'how their relation with one another determines the functional value of the whole.'[5]

Approach

His approach was moderated by his treatment of religion as 'a civilizing agency among the forces of historical evolution'.[6] He believed that Divine Revelation ('Wahi'), on which a religion

---

[1] See 'Islam as A Moral and Political Ideal' in Iqbal (1977/1995), pp.97-117
[2] Iqbal (1977/1995), pp.97-98
[3] Iqbal (1977/1995), p.98
[4] Iqbal (1977/1995), p.98
[5] Iqbal (1977/1995), p.98
[6] Iqbal (1977/1995), p.98

was based, was essentially a case of inspiration 'according to the needs of the recipient, or the needs of the species to which the recipient belongs'.[1]

Key questions

The new framework could be used for answering general questions about the role of Islam in human civilization as well as questions that were specific to the Muslims of British India.

General questions could include those raised by a critical student of religion with regard to the origin, growth and formation of a religious system from the standpoint of history. Questions specific to the Indian Muslims included some that would gradually become intimately relevant to others too, e.g.:

- Does the idea of Caliphate in Islam embody a religious institution?
- What is the real meaning of the doctrine of Jihad in Islam?
- What is the meaning of the expression 'from amongst you' in the Quranic verse: 'Obey God, obey the Prophet and the masters of the affairs (i.e. rulers) from amongst you?'
- What is the character of the traditions of the Prophet foretelling the advent of Imam Mehdi?[2]

He had an edge over rival thinkers from other cultures, such as modern Western thinkers, as he did not have to begin from the scratch. Muslims across the globe were already in agreement with him in principle. Just a suggestion from him could be

---

[1] The same phenomenon of Nature which made a plant grow freely in space, or an animal develop a new organism to suit a new environment, led to the birth of world religions in human beings. See Lecture V in Iqbal (1930/1934), p.119
[2] Iqbal (1977/1995), p.225

accepted by his society more readily than conclusive arguments from Western thinkers by theirs.

On the flipside, he was not going to be able to present his ideas as methodically as his Western counterparts, since he was not at liberty to do away with the deepest convictions of his people and build his system on completely new foundations.[1] He regarded this constraint as an opportunity, as evident from the thoughts he shared with fellow reformers of the Muslim world:

> ... it is absolutely necessary for these political reformers to make a thorough study of Islamic constitutional principles, and not to shock the naturally suspicious conservatism of their people by appearing as prophets of a new culture. They would certainly impress them more if they could show that their seemingly borrowed ideal of political freedom is really the ideal of Islam, and is, as such, the rightful demand of free Muslim conscience.[2]

'Political Thought in Islam' (1908)

The excerpt quoted above comes from 'Political Thought in Islam', the first of the three papers in which the new framework was laid out.[3] It was published in the third issue of *Sociological Review,* the new quarterly of London University.

This paper may truly be seen as the beginning of the thirty-year-long process about which it has been said that Iqbal cleared

---

[1] It has been observed that 'a planned and scientific speculative effort in political thought is not discernible' in Iqbal but 'his ideas and reflections, integrated in the light of his religious and philosophic background, form a compact and coherent scheme of thought leading to the emergence of an ideal political system'. See Dr. Parveen Shaukat Ali (1978), p.347
[2] Iqbal (1977/1995), 154
[3] Included in Iqbal (1977/1995), pp.138-154

'the debris of centuries of superimposed interpretations of jurists, mystics and commentators' and 'rediscovered the sterling principles' of Quranic precepts.[1]

Although in this first paper he dealt mainly with historical schools of Muslim political theory – Sunni, Shia and Khawarij – which had already become obsolete, it could still serve as a foundation stone for the future development of political thought in the world of Islam, as it traced the development of Muslim political thought up to that point and highlighted the approach, fundamental principles and basic tenets that had guided its development.

Significantly, he pointed out that the approach of the constitutional lawyers of Islam comprised of 'reflective criticism on the revelations of political experience.'[2]

The fundamental principles of Muslim constitutional theory were two: (a) political sovereignty *de facto* resided in the people; and (b) the idea of universal agreement.[3] Both principles could be traced back to the Quran and the practice of the Prophet, and were clearly implied by the second caliph, Umar al-Farooq, who said: 'An election which is only a partial expression of a people's will is null and void.'[1]

The two basic tenets of Muslim political thought were: (a) absolute equality of all citizens in the eye of the law; and (b) no

---

[1] Dr. Parveen Shaukat Ali (1978), p.351

[2] Iqbal (1977/1995), p.139

[3] This could also point to the difference with Western democracy. The ideal of Western democracy has been summarized as 'that sometimes we bow to the will of the majority. In doing that, we do not give up our convictions...' (See the speech by Eleanor Roosevelt, 'On the Adoption of the Universal Declaration of Human Rights', delivered 9 December 1948 in Paris, France. Retrieved on November 19, 2013). This was soon going to be labelled 'old democracy' by those thinkers who made the idea of universal agreement the cornerstone of the concept of a 'new democracy', passionately explained in *The New State* (1918) by Mary Parker Follett, which was indirectly mentioned by Iqbal in a letter dated January 6, 1923.

distinction between the Church and the State, and this meant that the state was free from the rule of priests.[2] In the exceptional case where the separation of church and state was effected, i.e. through the Shia doctrine of the Major Occultation of the Imam, it limited the authority of the Shah of Persia by the authority of the Mullas rather than the other way around (and Iqbal observed that 'the Mullas took an active part in the recent constitutional reforms in Persia').[3]

Implied here, but explained later, was the argument that separation of Church and state in a Muslim majority state was bound to be different from what it was in Christianity or modern West: 'the former is only a division of functions' whereas 'the latter is based on the metaphysical dualism of spirit and matter.'[4] After all, even if a Muslim majority state claimed to be secular, how could that mean 'the freedom of Muslim legislative activity from the conscience of the people which has for centuries been trained and developed by the spirituality of Islam'?[5]

Return to India

Around the time when the above-mentioned paper came out in July 1908, Iqbal was embarking on the return journey to British India via France. He wrote a grand poem, 'Sicily', on board the steamer.

He arrived in Bombay on July 25, and boarded a train for Delhi. On many of the stops on the way, he was greeted by

---

[1] Iqbal (1977/1995), p.139
[2] Iqbal (1977/1995), p.140-142. It was implied, although not stated, that the civil liberties which European states were seeking through separation of Church and state could be achieved in the world of Islam through the opposite.
[3] Iqbal (1977/1995), p.151
[4] Iqbal (1977/1995), p.235-236
[5] Iqbal (1977/1995), p.236

school children singing his famous patriotic poem, '*Saray jahan se achha Hindustan hamara.*' He arrived in Lahore on July 27, where friends and admirers gave him a grand reception.[1]

The next five years in his life could be divided into four areas: (a) teething problems of the new career as a barrister; (b) developing the new approach in his thought; (c) composition of private and public poetry; and (d) personal problems arising from irreconcilable differences with wife, and from his desire to get remarried.

Private poems

Many of the poems that he wrote around this time became too 'private', as he mentioned to Atiya Fyzee in a letter written on July 7, 1911: 'During the [last] 5, 6 years my poems have become more of a private nature and I believe the public have no right to read them. Some of them I have destroyed altogether for fear of somebody stealing them away and publishing them.'[2]

Fortunately, some of those poems survived, and a few were even included in his Urdu anthology later on.[3] It is possible to reconstruct through them the story of a young man wandering in the world in search of beauty, and suddenly finding himself in the presence of a beloved – and the chronology of the poems leaves no doubt that the object of this unmatched admiration was Emma Wegenast: 'Just as the silver boat of the moon sinks in the storm of sunlight in the early hours of dawn; just as the moon-coloured lotus disappears with a veil of illumination in the moonlit night; so is my heart in the deluge of your love.'[4] The

---

[1] Shafique (Urdu; 2010), pp.221-223
[2] B. A. Dar, Ed. (1978), p.36
[3] They were included in the second section of *The Call of the Marching Bell* (1924), i.e. Iqbal (Urdu; 1973), pp.109-142 [or Iqbal (Urdu; 1990), p.135-168]
[4] Translated from Iqbal (Urdu; 1973), p.116; [or Iqbal (Urdu; 1990), p.141-142]

sage also includes the poem 'An Evening', whose German translation is now inscribed on the bank of the River Necker in Heidelberg where the poet wrote it in the summer of 1907.[1]

These overwhelming sensations of an all-powerful love give way to excruciating pain of separation, which gradually leads the poet to a realization of an inherent unity in the seeming contradictions of his nature turns the psychological into the existential in 'The Inconstant Lover'. Private and public spheres then begin to merge. The dark night of the soul spreads out into the world – far-off lights of Sicily glimmer across a dark ocean, the entire Muslim world looks desolate and lies in ruins, and a forlorn moon watches over the crumbling tombs of dead kings.[2]

Completing the framework

His personal problems, which caused some of his poems to become too 'private', did not affect the development of his thought. Having laid down the foundations of his new framework in the paper published from London in July 1908, he continued working on it and completed it through two more papers and several 'public' poems.

'Islam as A Moral and Political Ideal' (1909)

Before leaving for Europe, he had been reciting at least one grand poem in the annual session of the philanthropic organization Anjuman Himayat-i-Islam, Lahore, every year. Apparently because he wanted to be heard as a thinker and messenger now rather than a mere poet, he refrained from

---

[1] The poem appears in Iqbal (Urdu; 1973), p.128; [or Iqbal (Urdu; 1990), p.154-155]

[2] Iqbal (Urdu; 1973), pp.129-148 [or, Iqbal (Urdu; 1990), p.155-174]

reciting any poem in the first annual session of the organization after his return from Europe, which was held in the Easter break of 1909. Instead, he delivered a lecture in English. It was later published, apparently with some revisions, in two instalments in the *Hindustan Review,* Allahabad, in July and December 1909. The title was 'Islam as A Moral and Political Ideal'.[1]

The paper served two purposes. Firstly, it outlined his framework (which has already been discussed above). Secondly, it outlined the basic propositions of four major religions in the light of the new framework:

1. *Buddhism:* There is pain in Nature, and the human being regarded as an individual is evil. Therefore, salvation is inaction through which the self could be annihilated; renunciation of self and un-worldliness are the principle virtues.

2. *Zoroastrianism:* There is struggle in Nature, and the human being is a mixture of the struggling forces. Salvation, therefore, lies in the freedom to range oneself on the side of the powers of good, which will eventually prevail.

3. *Christianity:* There is sin in Nature, and the taint of sin is fatal to human being. Therefore, salvation requires the force of a supernatural redeemer.

4. *Islam:* There is fear in Nature, but human being is essentially good and peaceful. Therefore, salvation is freedom from fear and grief.[2]

---

[1] The paper is included in Iqbal (1977/1995), pp.97-117

[2] Iqbal (1977/1995), pp.100-101. An example given by Iqbal for this new status bestowed by Islam on human being is the anecdote in the Quran about the angels and the Devil being commanded by God to bow down before the newly created Adam (who had been regarded by previous scriptures as 'a little below the angels'); see Iqbal (1977/1995), p.102.

Regarding Islam, he drew four important conclusions about its religious system:

- the essential nature of human being consisted in 'will, not intellect or understanding.'[1] This was the basic premise on which all subsequent writings of Iqbal were going to be based.
- the basic propositions of Islam and of modern European civilization were practically the same, i.e. 'the possibility of the elimination of sin and pain from the evolutionary process, and faith in the natural goodness of man.' Modern European civilization had 'almost unconsciously recognized the truth of these propositions in spite of the religious system with which it is associated.'[2]
- the ethical ideal of Islam was 'a strong will in a strong body.'[3]
- the political ideal of Islam was representative government: 'Democracy, then, is the most important aspect of Islam regarded as a political ideal.'[4]

Stray Reflections

Apparently for collecting building blocks for further development of the framework, he kept a notebook with him through most of 1910, jotting down brief notes – ranging from just a sentence to a page or two. On the first page he wrote 'Stray Thoughts' and then changed it to 'Stray Reflections'. The page was dated '27th April 10.' Some of the reflections were used soon afterwards in the paper 'The Muslim Community – A

---

[1] Iqbal (1977/1995), p.102
[2] Iqbal (1977/1995), p.103
[3] Iqbal (1977/1995), p.106
[4] Iqbal (1977/1995), p.115

Sociological Study', while some others were published after minor revisions as 'Stray Thoughts' in *New Era,* a mouthpiece newspaper of Muslim nationalism in 1917. The complete notebook was edited and published posthumously in 1962, edited by Iqbal's younger son Dr. Javid Iqbal. Since 2006, it is being published in a revised edition with annotations by the present author.[1]

Some of the reflections seem to have been written in a kind of personal code, whose true meaning may only be discerned if every word and phrase were to be understood exactly as it existed in the mind of Iqbal:

- Art is a sacred lie.[2]
- My friends often ask me, 'Do you believe in the existence of God'? I think I am entitled to know the meaning of the terms used in this question before I answer it. My friends ought to explain to me what they mean by 'believe,' 'existence' and 'God', especially by the last two, if they want an answer to their question. I confess I do not understand these terms; and whenever I cross-examine them I find that they do not understand them either.[3]

One of the most interesting strands of reflections was the role assigned to each nation in 'the economy of nature'.[4] Nations mentioned in the notebook were the Germans,[5] British,[6]

---

[1] See Iqbal (1961/2006).
[2] Iqbal (1961/2006), p.15
[3] Iqbal (1961/2006), p.19
[4] Iqbal (1961/2006), p.38. It would be interesting to compare the idea with the views expressed in the famous work, *On the Economy of Nations* (1842), by John Shore: 'How admirably every step in the human career will be found adapted, not only to its own end, but to the designs of providence...' (p.5)
[5] Iqbal (1961/2006), p.38
[6] Iqbal (1961/2006), p.133

Mexicans,[1] Persians,[2] Afghanistan,[3] the Indian Muslims[4] and the modern Hindu.[5] Most of these were later taken up for elaboration in other works, with some additions, most notably the Americans,[6] Italy,[7] France,[8] Russia,[9] Turkey,[10] Palestine,[11] Arabia,[12] Central Asian states[13] and African Muslims.[14]

Reflecting on his own community, he noted that government was 'one of the determining forces of a people's character'. Since their political fall, the Muslims of India had become 'probably the meanest' of all Muslim communities 'in point of character'. He went on to observe:

> I am almost a fatalist in regard to the various forces that ultimately decide the destinies of nations. As a political force we are perhaps no longer required; but we are, I believe, still indispensable to the world as the only testimony to the absolute Unity of God – Our value among nations, then, is purely evidential.[15]

His perception of his community as 'the only testimony to the absolute Unity of God' apparently represented the same current

---

[1] Iqbal (1961/2006), p.51
[2] Iqbal (1961/2006), p.49
[3] Iqbal (1961/2006), p.41
[4] Iqbal (1961/2006), p.27
[5] Iqbal (1961/2006), p.39
[6] The Urdu preface in Iqbal (Persian; 1973), p.182
[7] Shafique (Urdu; 2012), pp.429-430
[8] Shafique (Urdu; 2012), pp.429-430
[9] Shafique (Urdu; 2012), pp.429-430
[10] The poem 'The Dawn of Islam' in Iqbal (Urdu; 1973), pp.267-276 [or Iqbal (Urdu; 1990), p.281-291]
[11] The poem 'To the Palestinian Arab' in Iqbal (Urdu; 1973), p.261-262 [or Iqbal (Urdu; 1990), p.671]
[12] Various poems addressed to the Arabs in Iqbal (Persian; 1973), pp.963-973
[13] Iqbal (1977/1995), pp.273-276
[14] In the poem 'The Answer to the Complaint' in Iqbal (Urdu; 1973), p.207 [or Iqbal (Urdu; 1990), p.237]
[15] Iqbal (1961/2006), p.27

of thought that later made him propose and predict the birth of a new state as 'the final destiny' of the same community.[1]

In this reflection may also be discerned an echo of what he had said about the Indians in his famous national song *('Saray jahan se...')* in 1904: *'There must be something which has sustained us against centuries of hostile calamities.'* At that time, he was obviously thinking of Hindus as willing partners in unlocking such mysteries, but events had led him to believe that the entire soul of the modern Hindu had been seized by the ideal of political freedom, which was 'an absolutely new experience to him ... turning the various streams of his energy from their wonted channels and bringing them to force into this new channel of activity'. His prediction was:

> When he has passed through this experience he will realise his loss. He will be transformed into an absolutely new people – new in the sense that he will no longer find himself dominated by the ethical ideals of his ancestors whose sublime fancies have been a source of perpetual consolation to many a distressed mind.[2]

'The Muslim Community...' (1911)

Mohammedan Anglo-Oriental College had been founded by Sir Syed Ahmad Khan in 1877. He envisaged it as an independent university, since he believed political freedom to be a mere illusion without freedom of education. Unfortunately, the charter of university had been denied it by the British rulers so far. By 1909, the demand for a Muslim University was afloat again (it would be granted eventually in 1922, but on terms and

---

[1] In the *Allahabad Address;* see Shafique (2006/2007), pp.139
[2] Iqbal (1961/2006), p.39

conditions that would be a far cry from the vision of its pioneer). Iqbal was involved in the deliberations about the Muslim University, and was invited for an extensive lecture at Aligarh on February 9, 1911.[1] The lecture, 'The Muslim Community – A Sociological Study', completed the basic framework of his thought by providing (a) a general conception of society; (b) the specific structure of Muslim society; and (c) the ideal to be desired by this society in the present times.

Iqbal mentioned what Post-Darwinian biology had to say about the general conception of society, but attempted to go beyond the existing concepts like public opinion, national genius or Zeitgeist, while proposing that 'society has or rather tends to have a consciousness, a will, and an intellect of its own, though the stream of its mentality has no other channel through which to flow than individual minds.'[2]

Regarding the specific structure of the Muslim society, he showed it to be ultimately determined by the religious idea 'without any theological centralisation, which would unnecessarily limit the liberty of the individual.'[3] The membership of this society comprised of shared belief in a certain view of the universe and participation in the same historical tradition. This was unlike other societies where

---

[1] Shafique (Urdu; 2010), p.346

[2] Iqbal (1977/1995), p.119. The three traits listed here – consciousness, will and intellect – offered a rare combination. Rousseau had placed emphasis on general will but the concepts of collective consciousness and collective intellect became popular much later, and were often used as substitutes for Rousseau's general will (as the young Carl Jung had just started to do in Germany around this time). It seems that by starting with the premise that the essential nature of human being consists in will, it became natural for Iqbal to arrive at the conception of a collective organism which included all three, i.e. will, intellect and consciousness (understanding).

[3] Iqbal (1977/1995), p.123

nationality comprised of 'the unity of language or country or the identity of economic interest'.[1]

The ideal sought by such a society should be the development of a specific type of character in accordance with the evolutionary needs of the society. These had been described by the American sociologist Franklin Henry Gidding in the *Inductive Sociology* (1901) to be basically four:

1. *The Forceful:*[2] someone in whom the qualities of courage and power are emphasized becomes popular in primitive societies where the struggle for existence draws more upon physical rather than intellectual qualities. Iqbal called it 'the valiant' type, and identified Tamerlane as representing this type in the evolution of the Muslim community in India.[3]

2. *The Convivial:*[4] this type becomes popular when the struggle for existence relaxes and the community does not face an imminent threat of extinction anymore. Now admiration turns to those who take a due share in all the pleasures of life, and combine in themselves the virtues of liberality, generosity and good fellowship. Iqbal identified Emperor Babur as combining the first and the second types, and Emperor Jahangir as embodying predominantly the second.[5]

3. *The Austere:*[6] As a reaction against the tendencies to become reckless, which are found in the first two types, a great type of character emerges, holding up the ideal of self-control and dominated by a more serious view of

---

[1] Iqbal (1977/1995), p.121
[2] Gidding (1901), p.82
[3] Iqbal (1977/1995), p.127
[4] Gidding (1901), p.83
[5] Iqbal (1977/1995), p.127
[6] Gidding (1901), p.83

life. According to Iqbal, this type was 'foreshadowed' in Emperor Aurangzeb Alamgir.[1]

4. *The Rationally Conscientious:*[2] A reaction against, and progress beyond, the austere type of character often transforms the austere type into 'rationally conscientious', with a broadening of views and an increased emphasis on a complete development of all powers of mind and body. Iqbal did not mention this type in his paper.

Iqbal upheld the austere type as 'the Muslim type of character' and proposed that all education in the Muslim community should aim at developing this type of character.[3] Later on, he would propose the same aim for art and literature, and would offer a complete programme to this end in the first book of poetry, *Secrets and Mysteries.*

The idea of a university

He believed that modern education was insufficient for developing the austere type of character because it proceeded 'on the false assumption' that the idea of education is the training of human intellect rather than human will.[4] He found technical education to be more important for this purpose than higher education, since 'education, like other things, ought to be determined by the needs of the learner; ... [i.e.] the particular type of character which you want to develop'.[5]

---

[1] Iqbal (1977/1995), p.127
[2] Gidding (1901), p.83
[3] Iqbal (1977/1995), p.127
[4] Iqbal (1977/1995), p.110
[5] Iqbal (1977/1995), p.109

He believed that education should be 'a deliberate effort to bring about an organic relation between the individual and the body-politic to which he belongs.'[1]

The object of education should be to secure orderly transmission of the collective experience of the social mind – or the collective ego of a society – from generation to generation. Disruption in this orderly transmission could create illness in the collective mind of the society, just as disturbance in the continuity of the stream of individual consciousness results in psychic ill health 'which may, in course of time, lead on to a final dissolution of vital forces.'[2]

As far as higher education was concerned, he believed that a university should have two major purposes:

a. it should enable the learners to keep pace with the progress of modern ideas while retaining the distinct character of their culture; and

b. it should organize the scattered educational forces of society into a central institution of a large purpose.

For his community, he believed that a Muslim University was needed so that it could end the dichotomy between modern education and religious education. It should bring together 'the Nadwa, the Aligarh College, the theological Seminary of Deoband, and other institutions of a similar type' and 'afford opportunities not only for the development of special abilities, but may also create the necessary type of culture for the modern Indian Muslim.'[3] Therefore, he proposed:

A purely Western ideal of education will be dangerous to the life of our community ... It is therefore absolutely necessary to construct a fresh educational

---

[1] Iqbal (1977/1995), p.130
[2] Iqbal (1977/1995), p.130
[3] Iqbal (1977/1995), p.133

ideal in which the elements of Muslim culture must find a prominent place, and past and the present commingle in a happy union. The construction of such an ideal is not an easy task; it requires a large imagination, a keen perception of the tendencies of modern times, and a complete grasp of the meaning of Muslim history and religion.[1]

Poems of Muslim nationalism

As mentioned earlier, he had been reluctant to recite poetry in public gatherings ever since his return from Europe. Having completed his new framework in March 1911, he broke his silence with 'The Complaint', recited in the annual session of the Anjuman in April 1911.[2] Then there was no holding him back, and this period witnessed the birth of those poems that turned Iqbal into a unique phenomenon in the history of Islam – 'The Complaint',[3] 'Fatima Bint-i-Abdullah',[4] 'Prayer',[5] 'The Anthem of the Muslim Nation',[6] 'The Candle and the Poet',[7] 'In the Presence of the Holy Prophet',[8] 'The Answer to the Complaint'[9] and so on.

Most of these poems were inspired by political events of the times, especially the Italian invasion of Tripoli in 1911, and the Balkan War in 1912. They revealed two major implications of his new approach. The first was that some of the expressions

---

[1] Iqbal (1977/1995), p.133
[2] Shafique (Urdu; 2010), pp.367-369
[3] Iqbal (Urdu; 1973), pp.163-170 [or Iqbal (Urdu; 1990), p.190-199]
[4] Iqbal (Urdu; 1973), pp.214-215 [or Iqbal (Urdu; 1990), p.243-244]
[5] Iqbal (Urdu; 1973), pp.212-213 [or Iqbal (Urdu; 1990), p.241-242]
[6] Iqbal (Urdu; 1973), p.159 [or Iqbal (Urdu; 1990), p.186]
[7] Iqbal (Urdu; 1973), pp.183-195 [or Iqbal (Urdu; 1990), p.210-222]
[8] Iqbal (Urdu; 1973), p.214 [or Iqbal (Urdu; 1990), p.224-225]
[9] Iqbal (Urdu; 1973), pp.199-208 [or Iqbal (Urdu; 1990), p.227-237]

conventionally reserved for alluding to the Divine Being were now applied to the collective entity of community, e.g. 'The existence of individuals is virtual; the life of the nation is real.'[1]

The other implication was his outburst against territorial nationalism. The homelands of modern nations appeared to him like so many idols for so many tribes – Germany for Germans, Britain for British, and so on. 'The idol-maker of civilization has presented new idols in this age,' he declared in the poem, 'Patriotism'. 'Chief among these new idols is country...' He implored his Muslim audience to break this idol, and to make Islam their homeland.[2]

Despair, anger and disillusionment from personal life may have become distilled with the political setbacks of the Muslim world, and produced that extraordinary pressure which resulted in the cathartic outcome of 'The Complaint' – his greatest poem until then, and one of his most famous ever. 'Your world presented a weird look until we arrived on the scene,' he dared say to the Almighty while petitioning on behalf of the Muslim nation.[3] Why, then, the Divine Benevolence seemed to be reserved exclusively for non-Muslims today? Still, the poem was essentially a prayer, and celebrated the bonding between the human soul and the Creator: 'Allow the song of this solitary nightingale to pierce through the hearts of the listeners! Let the call of this marching bell awaken the hearts from deep slumber, and be freshened up with a new covenant but thirsting for the same old wine.'[4]

In poems inspired by contemporary setbacks to Muslim power, spontaneous expression of grief was invariably superseded by the acute self-awareness of the poet of being a

---

[1] Iqbal (Urdu; 1973), p.130 [or Iqbal (Urdu; 1990), p.156]
[2] Iqbal (Urdu; 1973), p.160-161 [or Iqbal (Urdu; 1990), p.187-188]
[3] Iqbal (Urdu; 1973), p.163 [or Iqbal (Urdu; 1990), p.191]
[4] Iqbal (Urdu; 1973), p.170 [or Iqbal (Urdu; 1990), p.1198-199]

visionary who could see beyond the apparent. In his private correspondence, he made no secret of the fact that he believed himself to have a keen insight into the destiny of nations, and that some of his poems were intended to be prophesies. 'I have written a few verses at the end [of that poem], which have been corroborated by the [breaking out of] the war between Turkey and Italy,' he wrote on October 6, 1911, to the senior poet Akbar Allahabadi, whom he had begun to see as a kind of mentor.

Sirdar Begum

The issues in his personal life finally came to resolution in the summer of 1913.

Since his return in 1908, he had been striving to resettle, and at one time he even entertained the idea of settling abroad – possibly with Emma. In stark contrast to the notes made in his private notebook, and the views expressed in his public writings, he would sometimes 'disburden'[1] his soul in his private correspondence with Atiya Fyzee, especially in the years 1909-11. 'A good God created all this, you will say,' he had written in the letter dated April 9, 1909, 'May be. The facts of this life, however, tend to a different conclusion. It is intellectually easier to believe in an eternal omnipotent Devil rather than a good God.'[2] Yet, the views expressed so flippantly in private correspondence seem to be grounded in some well-considered thoughts, such as those expressed around the same time in the paper 'Islam as A Moral and Political Ideal':

I hope I shall not be offending the reader when I say that I have a certain amount of admiration for the

---

[1] B. A. Dar, Ed. (1978), p.22
[2] B. A. Dar, Ed. (1978), pp.21-22

devil. By refusing to prostrate himself before Adam whom he honestly believed to be his inferior, he revealed a high sense of self-respect ... And I believe God punished him not because he refused to make himself low before the progenitor of an enfeebled humanity, but because he declined to give absolute obedience to the will of the Almighty Ruler of the Universe.[1]

Eventually he reconciled with the idea of settling down in British India – either due to his higher calling or because his elder brother was going to be retired in two years' time and would need him, having sponsored his education so generously.[2] In the winter of 1910, Iqbal got remarried – almost. He had allowed his mother to choose the bride (although only after seeing a picture of hers). Sirdar Begum, the bride, was around eighteen at the time, and came from a humble family of Kashmiri origins living in Lahore. She was an orphan and had one brother. After the pronouncement of the marriage (*nikah*), and before the groom could be joined by the bride a few days later in the ceremony of *rukhsati,* he started receiving anonymous letters casting doubt on her character.[1]

Consequently, he gave up the idea of going through with this marriage. Another wife was found for him in the first half of 1913. She was Mukhtar Begum, the orphaned niece of a well-to-do gentleman from Ludhiana, a town in the Eastern part of Punjab. She was of an amiable nature and was fond of keeping pets, especially a cat.

Soon afterwards, it was found that the anonymous letters against Sirdar had been written maliciously by the father of a rejected suitor. The young woman herself wrote to her husband

---

[1] Iqbal (1977/1995), p.107-108
[2] Shafique (Urdu; 2010), p.224

at this point, frankly accusing him of a wrong judgement that had destroyed her life.[2] He was deeply moved – 'it's a strange love story,' he wrote to a friend shortly afterwards.[3] With the full consent of Mukhtar, he brought Sirdar to his home as his third wife.[4]

Karim Bibi, the estranged first wife, had requested not to be divorced. As mentioned earlier, she lived in separation for the rest of her life, receiving a monthly stipend from her husband and surviving him by nine years.[5] Mukhtar died in childbirth in 1924.[6] Sirdar gave birth to a son, Javid, in 1924,[7] and a daughter, Munira, in 1930.[8] Sirdar died in 1935.[9] Iqbal remained fond of her as long as she lived, and even afterwards. 'Her soul is in contact with me', he is reported to have said sometime after her death.[10]

It may also be significant that it was only after marrying Sirdar that Iqbal was finally able to take up the long-delayed project of writing a long Persian poem for expounding his system of thought. The poem, *Secrets and Mysteries,* was completed while the world around him was engaged in the conflict that was perceived by many of his readers as a partial fulfilment of the prophecies he had made in the poem 'March 1907', seven years earlier.

---

[1] Dr. Javid Iqbal (Urdu; 2008), p.204
[2] Dr. Javid Iqbal (Urdu; 2008), p.204
[3] Iqbal's letter to Kishan Prashad dated October 26, 1913. Quoted in Shafique (Urdu; 2010).
[4] Dr. Javid Iqbal (Urdu; 2008), p.204
[5] Dr. Javid Iqbal (Urdu; 2008), p.195
[6] Dr. Javid Iqbal (Urdu; 2008), p.345
[7] Dr. Javid Iqbal (Urdu; 2008), p.345
[8] Shafique (2006/2007), p.115
[9] Dr. Javid Iqbal (Urdu; 2008), pp.607-608
[10] See Niazi (1971)

The Great European War

On the morning of June 28, 1914, in Sarajevo, the twenty-year-old Bosnian Serb Gavrilo Princip emerged from Moritz Schiller's café moments before the motorcade of the visiting prince of Austria-Hungary entered the street after taking a wrong turn. Princip rushed forward to fire two shots with his .380 FN semi-automatic pistol. The prince and his wife died before medical help could be given.

In the aftermath, Austria-Hungary blamed Serbia for supporting terrorism and treaties signed between the various countries of Europe with the aim of securing peace became the instruments through which the entire continent was plunged into a 'Great War', coming suicide with its own dagger as prophesied by Iqbal.[1]

Throughout the four years of the Great European War – 1914 to 1918 – the poet-philosopher remained preoccupied with the writing of a long poem expounding his approach to life,[2] and earning his livelihood through the unrelated activities of legal practice and checking answer books for universities.

'In Memoriam of the Late Mother' (1915)

His mother, Imam Bibi, died in Sialkot on November 9, 1914.[3] Iqbal felt the blow like a child. 'My interest in the worldly matters and my urge to be successful in life was due only to her,' he wrote in a letter. 'Now I am just awaiting my death...'[4]

---

[1] Many contemporaries of Iqbal treated World War I as a fulfillment of this prophecy. See, for instance, Khan (1922/1982), p.13
[2] *Secrets and Mysteries,* published in installments between 1915 and 1922
[3] Shafique (Urdu; 2012), p.72
[4] Letter to Kishan Prashad, dated November 23, 1914, quoted in Shafique (Urdu; 2012), p.80

However, he continued working on the first part of *Secrets and Mysteries* until it was finished sometime in July the next year. Prolonged grief, remarkably sustained, then burst forth as one of his longer poems in Urdu, 'In Memoriam of the Late Mother', written in August 1915.[1]

Significantly, it was his first long poem in Urdu that was not meant for recital in a large crowd. Mellow tone, gentle rhythm and frank expressions of personal grief made the poem stand apart from most of his other poetical work. The argument of poem moved from personal recollections of motherly love to general observations about the abundance of death and the even greater abundance of the life instinct. Existence, rather than non-existence, was ultimately shown to be the Nature's favourite, and hence the possibility of life after death became self-evident. The conclusion comprised of a brief prayer that soon became proverbial in the Urdu speaking world, and still remains one of the most common epitaphs on tombstones in the region: 'May the sky shed dewdrops on your grave. May this abode be guarded ever by new blossoms.'[2]

آسماں تیری لحد پر شبنم افشانی کرے

سبزہ ء نورُستہ اِس گھر کی نگہبانی کرے

Although prompted by a personal loss, the theme of the poem coincided with the most popular poems that were being written elsewhere in the world, having death and mourning as their dominant themes due to the Great European War.

---

[1] Anthologized in Iqbal (Urdu; 1973), pp.226-236 [or Iqbal (Urdu; 1990), p.254-266]. For biographical background, see Shafique (Urdu;2012), pp.131-154.

[2] Iqbal (Urdu; 1973), p.236. [or Iqbal (Urdu; 1990), p.266]

Secrets and Mysteries (1915-22)

The need for the world to resurrect itself after the catastrophe of the Great European War was addressed from an essentially Muslim point of view in the long philosophical poem completed by Iqbal during the war years. *Secrets and Mysteries* (Asrar-o-Ramooz) turned out to be the first complete book of his poetry. It was in Persian, and was self-published from Lahore in two instalments – 'Secrets of the Self' (Asrar-i-Khudi) in September 1915 and 'Mysteries of Selflessness' (Ramooz-i-Bekhudi) in April 1918. The complete edition was self-published in 1922 (or possibly 1923) as *Secrets and Mysteries.*[1] A third part was also initiated with the working title of 'The Future History of the Muslim Nation'.[2] It got delayed by several years and while most biographers of Iqbal believe that he never completed it, it is quite possible that his greatest masterpiece *Javid Nama* (1932) was actually a much evolved form of the same.[3]

He claimed that *Secrets and Mysteries* was inspired by the appearance of the 13th Century Sufi Maulana Jalaluddin Rumi in a dream. The author of the great *Masnavi* and *Divan-i-Shams Tabriz* asked him to write a *masnavi* too, and he woke up writing Persian verses although he had written very little in that language until then.[4] He eventually became the greatest modern poet of Persian without being able to speak the language fluently till the very end. Rumi remained his mentor forever after, and reappeared in each of the subsequent books of his poetry.[5]

---

[1] Now included in Iqbal (Persian; 1973), pp.1-170. For publication history, see Shafique (2006/2007), pp.84-85 and Hashmi (Urdu; 1982/2010), p.125.
[2] Shafique (Urdu; 2009), p.310
[3] See the section 'Javid Nama' in Chapter 5.
[4] Shafique (Urdu; 2010), pp.460-462
[5] Iqbal is now widely regarded as the foremost modern disciple of Rumi, and even has a symbolic grave inside the compound of Rumi's mausoleum in Konya (Turkey). In the international conference organized by UNESCO on the

His interpretation of Rumi was, however, based on an understanding that the spirit of Devotional Sufism (represented by Rumi, Bu Ali Qalandar, Nizamuddin Aulya, Mian Mir and others) was not necessarily the same as that of metaphysical mysticism (such as Ibn-ul-Arabi and Al-Jili).[1] Iqbal's understanding of Rumi was, therefore, independent of classical interpretations of the master. Also, a Persian masnavi written by a master of Devotional Sufism from the 14th Century India, Bu Ali Qalandar, was yet another role model that Iqbal had used as a role model for his own work.[2]

Iqbal's masnavi presented his previously explained framework in the form of a handbook for developing the austere type of character – which had been declared by him to be the most important need of his community – but it also introduced three new concepts to the previously explained framework. These were (a) a unique conception of the soul as ego; (b) a reinterpretation of three universal principles, i.e. solidarity, equality and freedom; and (c) a manifesto for art and literature. In this way, it also became the first coherent exposition of Muslim nationalism, which was much needed but unavailable at that time. This is may explain why the book became a phenomenon across the Muslim world within a few years of its publication – and remained so until 1953, when it was singled out by a Cambridge Orientalist as the most potent threat to Western supremacy.[3] Appealing primarily to will rather than intellect, the book employed parables, articles of faith, verses of the Quran, sayings of the Prophet, and allusions to famous

---

eighth birth centenary of Rumi, papers about Iqbal were also admitted freely on the ground that his work was legitimately a part of Rumi's legacy.
[1] E.g., 'Devotional Sufism alone tried to understand the meaning of the unity of inner experience...' Lecture IV in Iqbal (1930/1934), p.91
[2] B. A. Dar, Ed. (1978), p.36
[3] This is a reference to A. J. Aberry. See the preface of his translation of the second part of the book as 'Mysteries of Selflessness', published in 1953.

historical personalities. Its remarkably symmetrical structure made it handy and compact, and also quite attractive.[1]

The book was also an apt introduction of Iqbal as a seer and a visionary. Declaring himself 'the voice of the Poet of Tomorrow', he addressed the future generations: 'My own age does not know the secrets. My Joseph is not for this market.'[2] In the epilogue, he revealed the source of his wisdom when he addressed the Prophet and urged: 'If the essence of my word is anything but the Quran, choke in my breast the narrow breath of life and guard your people against the mischief of my wickedness. But if I have threaded on my chain the pearl of the mysteries of the Quran, plead to God my cause'.[3]

Ego

A unified and comprehensive conception of personality – which, according to a modern writer 'is what the Western writers have yearned for' – was the first of the three new storeys now added to the gradually rising edifice of Iqbal's thought.[4]

The expression 'ego' (*khudi* in Urdu and Persian) was used by him for referring to the self, which he perceived as 'a unity of life'. He defined it as 'the unity of human consciousness which constitutes the centre of human personality'.[5] Depending on one's point of view, it could be perceived as feeling, self-identity, soul or will.[6]

Objectively, it could not be regarded as more than 'the finite centre of experience'.[7] Understandably, some ancient

---

[1] For the internal coherence of the poem, see Shafique (2007/2009), pp. 23-38
[2] Iqbal (Persian; 1973), p.6
[3] Iqbal (Persian; 1973), p.168
[4] The quotation is from Qaiser (1994), p.78
[5] Lecture IV, in Iqbal (1930/1934), p.90.
[6] Lecture IV, in Iqbal (1930/1934), p.93
[7] Lecture IV, in Iqbal (1930/1934), p.93

doctrines, such as Hinduism, and pre-Islamic religions, such as Buddhism, had treated it either as an illusion or as something that should be extinguished in any case. To them, the only ego that really existed was the world-soul, cosmic mind or cosmic consciousness, i.e. God. Modern European philosophy preached likewise, despite having a very different outlook from that of the ancient beliefs.[1] In the 1880s and the 1890s, British philosopher F. C. Bradley argued that reason could only accept an Absolute unity, in which the finite centres lose their finiteness and distinctness. The individual ego was not real, although it appeared 'in some sense real' and 'in some sense an indubitable fact'.[2] German philosopher Nietzsche also implied that ego was a fiction.[3]

Iqbal rejected the possibility of 'universal life' and insisted that all life is individual.[4] The Ultimate Reality (or God, in the language of religion) must also be conceived as an ego – the Ultimate Ego, and 'from the Ultimate Ego only egos proceed'. In the picture of Creation drawn on this basis, human being as an individual ego was nearer 'than his own neck-vein' to God, the Ultimate Ego.[5]

There were five major characteristics of the Ultimate Ego (or, five elements in the Islamic conception of God): (a) Intensive Infinity; (b) Creativity; (c) Knowledge; (d) Power; (e) Eternity.[6] Five characteristics of ego as manifested in human being were:

---

[1] In an Urdu essay in 1916, Iqbal observed that the 'intellectual creed' [*ilmi mazhab*] of Europe was pantheism. Quoted in Shafique (Urdu; 2012), p.209
[2] Quotations are from F.C. Bradley, cited in Lecture IV, Iqbal (1930/1934), p.93.
[3] 'An Exposition of the Self', notes dictated by Iqbal to Syed Nazeer Niazi in 1937, included in Iqbal (1979/2003), p.208.
[4] Notes from Iqbal in the introduction to *Secrets of the Self* (1920), included as 'The Basic Philosophy of Asrar-i-Khudi' in Iqbal (1979/2003), p.194
[5] Lecture III in Iqbal (1930/1934), p.68
[6] Lecture III in Iqbal (1930/1934), especially pp.59-61

a. it reveals itself as a unity of mental states;[1]
b. it is not space-bound 'in the sense in which the body is space bound';[2]
c. its time-span is also fundamentally different to the time-span of the physical event, which is stretched out in space as a present fact, whereas the ego's duration is concentrated within it and linked with its present and future in a unique manner;[3]
d. it has an essential privacy that reveals the uniqueness of every ego;[4] and
e. it is a directive energy, formed and disciplined by its own experience, which means that 'the life of the ego is a kind of tension caused by the ego invading the environment and the environment invading the ego'.[5]

This conception of ego as a directive energy opened up the possibility of a rational understanding of immortality, or life after death, which could now be studied as an experience analogous to the facts of history and Nature.[6]

This was a wholesale rejection of some deep-rooted concepts of the ancient and modern times. To the Muslim school of theology represented by Al-Ghazzali, ego was a soul-entity or an immutable substance. Many schools of Christianity, Judaism and Zoroastrianism conceived 'a structurally dualistic soul-picture', based on dichotomy between spirit and matter.[7] Modern

---

[1] Lecture IV in Iqbal (1930/1934), p.93
[2] Lecture IV, in Iqbal (1930/1934), p.94
[3] Lecture IV, in Iqbal (1930/1934), p.94
[4] Lecture IV, in Iqbal (1930/1934), p.94
[5] Lecture IV in Iqbal (1930/1934), p.97
[6] This is the topic of the latter part of Lecture IV, in Iqbal (1930/1934), pp.104-117
[7] Lecture IV, in Iqbal (1930/1934), p.91, 95. It has also been observed that 'a major contribution of Iqbal to Muslim thought consists in his attempt to break

psychology, finding no support in philosophy for the reality of ego, conceived it as 'part of the system of thought'[1] (and hence Sigmund Freud was also to define ego as a mental construct rather than an entity). New or old, these ideas were not compatible with the worldview of Iqbal.

Ideal principles

'The essence of "Tauhid" [the Unity of God] as a working idea, is equality, solidarity, and freedom'.[2] The concept was summarized in these words in a later writing, but was painstakingly elaborated in *Secrets and Mysteries,* showing that the mission of the Prophet of Islam was the propagation of these three ideal principles.[3]

This completed the earlier statements that the basic propositions of Islam and of modern European civilization were practically the same. In retrospect, it may be seen to negate the possibility of any 'clash of civilizations' by showing that the supposed goals of two major cultural forces – Islam and the modern West – is practically the same. What could bother the Western critics (and it did bother quite a few of them) was the fact that the book attempted to take each principle a step farther than the idealism of Europe:

> ▪ *Solidarity* was shown to require that even the opinions of the unaware and uninformed masses should be treated with the same respect as those of the more enlightened ones, provided that the result did not go against compassion. In the parable, a decision taken by

---

down the wall (erected by al-Ghazzali) between analytic thought and religious consciousness.' (Mir (2006), p.99)
[1] Lecture IV, in Iqbal (1930/1934), p.96
[2] Lecture VI, in Iqbal (1930/1934), p.147
[3] Iqbal (Persian; 1973), pp.103-111

an uninformed soldier of a Muslim army was upheld by the commander in chief above his own previous order, on the ground that the word of one Muslim was as good as another because they were all bonded by the love of the Prophet. Consequently, a condemned prisoner of war was spared his life, since he had received amnesty by the mistake of the low-ranking soldier.[1]

- *Equality* was traced to the fact that the law of the Quran was irrevocable and equally binding on everybody, regardless of their social status and power. The consequence was a balance between justice and mercy: a person whose hand was to be amputated according to law was spared his limb because the source of law, the Quran, had also decreed mercy and forgiveness.[2]

- *Freedom* was defined as the right of human being to bow before nobody except God, and hence an expression of love rather than desire for power, identified with principles and their long-term effect in the evolution of society. It was symbolized through Husain, the grandson of the Prophet, who laid down his life in defiance against hereditary monarchy when it appeared in Islam for the very first time. Thereby, the rule of acquiring throne directly through inheritance was rendered illegitimate in Islam forever, and not even the hand of Time was going to bring it back.[3]

A manifesto of art and literature

Secrets and Mysteries offered a program for the reform of Islamic literature, evidently based on the poetics of Hali. The

---

[1] Iqbal (Persian; 1973), pp.105-106
[2] Iqbal (Persian; 1973), pp.107-108
[3] Iqbal (Persian; 1973), pp.109-111

five most important aspects, including details that emerged later but were implied here, were:

1. Art and literature should strengthen the will of the audience through celebration of love and beauty, because the function of art and literature is to evoke desire for action.[1]

2. Art and literature employ symbols, even when this is not intended by the artist or writer, since 'inspiration is not a matter of choice. It is a gift...'[2] (Two symbols that came to represent the message of Iqbal were the tulip and the eagle).

3. Art and literature are like dreams that come true, because the character of the inspiration embodied in them 'cannot be critically judged by the recipient before accepting it'.[3] Yet, once accepted, they mould the will of the recipient. Therefore, 'Nations are born in the hearts of poets; they prosper and die in the hands of politicians'.[4]

4. Societies perish when they 'permit the visible to shape the invisible' by following pessimist artists and writers – described by Fichte as those who see all things 'thinner, smaller and emptier than they actually are'.[5]

5. The aim of art and literature should be to present ideals, i.e. to offer a vision of things as they ought to be, because 'both God and man live by perpetual creation'.[6] The most important ideal at least for the Muslims of India was the austere type of character.

---

[1] Iqbal (Persian; 1973), pp.34-39
[2] 'Foreword, *Muraqqa-i-Chughtai*' included in Iqbal (1979/2003), p.312
[3] 'Foreword, *Muraqqa-i-Chughtai*' included in Iqbal (1979/2003), p.312
[4] Iqbal (1961/2006), p.142
[5] Cited in 'Foreword, *Muraqqa-i-Chughtai*'; see Iqbal (1979/2003), p.313
[6] Iqbal, 'Foreword: *Muraqqa-i-Chughtai*' (1928) in Iqbal (1979/2003), p.313

Evils to be eradicated were mainly two: (a) complete un-worldliness, symbolized here by Plato; and (b) complete materialism, symbolized here by Machiavelli. The ancient Greek philosopher stood for 'those philosophical systems which hold up death rather than life as their ideal—systems which ignore the greatest obstruction to life, namely, matter, and teach us to run away from it instead of absorbing it'.[1] The Italian thinker of modern Europe represented the purely geographical conception of nationality along with its attendant materialism, which had led humanity to the brink of extinction.[2] The urgent task that Iqbal placed before the writers, artists and intellectuals was to rid the world of both these influences, which he considered to be equally dangerous although one had been passing as saintliness and the other as realism.

Mutual acceptance

To those who agreed with *Secrets and Mysteries,* its publication signified that the Indian Muslim community had come of age. It now had a worldview of its own, complete with a political philosophy that could be put to action. It was also observed that the enlightened outlook of modern writers among Arabs, Persians and Turks had remained necessarily restricted to their respective territories, but the Indian Muslims had presented a synthesis of modern ideas with the past, present and future of Islam as a cultural entity or a universal movement. They were alone in doing this, within the Muslim world or without.[3] With *Secrets and Mysteries,* they had finally produced something that

---

[1] Notes from Iqbal in the introduction to *Secrets of the Self* (1920), included as 'The Basic Philosophy of Asrar-i-Khudi' in Iqbal (1979/2003), p.196
[2] Iqbal (Persian; 1973), pp.115-117
[3] Syed Naseer Ahmad, B.A. (1935), p.32

could be offered to the Muslim world as a fresh interpretation of their common faith. It was based on universally shared ideal principles, without recourse to dogma, and could therefore be presented even to the people of the West as the next stage in the evolution of their own civilization.[1]

A critical mass of people began to see themselves as followers of Iqbal, and not just as his audience. Many had hailed Iqbal as their teacher long ago (including the journalist and political activist Muhammad Ali Jauhar since as early as 1912),[2] but the publication of the first instalment of *Secrets and Mysteries* in 1915 gave it a boost, and then there was no turning back. Intelligentsia came hand in hand with the unschooled masses, and the proclamation was so loud that its echo was heard even by the British literary critic Herbert Reed quoted a contemporary Muslim writer in 1921, 'Iqbal has come amongst us as a Messiah and has stirred the dead with life'.[3]

The extraordinary influence that Iqbal came to exercise on his community has been ascribed to the fact that his message comprised of:

> ... a direct appeal to the spark of honour, combined with religious fervour, that he knew still burnt in the heart of each individual member of his community. In words of gentle persuasion and high inspiration ... his voice reached ears which had long waited for such encouragement. The appeal was not only to the literary or the intellectual classes.[4]

---

[1] Referring to Iqbal and another writer, A.J. Arberry observed sarcastically in the preface of his translation of Iqbal's *Mysteries of Selflessness* (1953): 'Christian Europe, adventuring into the East upon its self-appointed civilizing mission, is now informed that it is itself in need of civilizing anew from the East.'
[2] See the section 'Muhammad Ali Jauhar'
[3] Quoted in Khan (1922/1982), p.16
[4] Justice A. R. Cornelius (2004), p.97

It also helped that he was ever so eager to respect the public opinion of his community – just like the army chief in his parable about 'solidarity', who preferred to take back his own order rather than supersede the word of an uninformed soldier. His handling of three of the issues touched upon in *Secrets and Mysteries* offered a good explanation of this approach.

Metaphysical mysticism

Iqbal believed that three evils had been responsible for the perils of the Muslim world: Mullaism, Mysticism and Kings (the last of these was replaced by feudal lords in British India). Picking up the campaign led against these by the 19th Century reformers, he criticized the doctrine of *wahdat al wujud* in the Urdu preface of the first edition of 'Secrets of the Self' (the first part of *Secrets and Mysteries*). This raised an outcry from the mystics, led by one of Iqbal's best friends, Hasan Nizami, who had been promoting the poem prior to its publication. Iqbal defended his position in a series of essays, but patched up with Nizami when the senior poet Akbar Allahabadi intervened with well-meaning satire against both contenders.[1]

Afterwards, Iqbal expunged the controversial passages from the next edition of the poem and also discouraged his followers from engaging in purely esoteric debates, saying that 'not only the masses but even the [intellectual] elite are not interested'.

Around this time, he also started writing a history of Sufism, tracing the development of Muslim metaphysical mysticism and its adverse impact on society. It could not be completed but a comparison of the unfinished draft with his later published work shows how generously he modified his views soon afterwards, and how willingly he accepted any fresh

---

[1] Shafique (Urdu; 2012), pp.204-5, 254

evidence which disproved any of his views.[1] In his poetry, he also continued employing imagery and notions from the conventional literature of *wahdat-al-wujud* as long as they could serve as vehicles for his thought.

Hafiz of Shiraz

The first edition of 'Secrets of the Self' also contained a criticism of the great Persian poet Hafiz of Shiraz, in the same chapter as Plato. It seems that the criticism was added to the chapter as an afterthought, basically stating that the poetry of Hafiz glorified weakness and weakened the will of the audience.[2] Since Hafiz was admired widely as a Sufi, a seer and a spiritual guide, Iqbal's criticism of him was met with such outrage that the entire book seemed to be in the danger of being condemned by a considerable number of enlightened readers.

In the midst of a heated and emotional debate, the scholar Ferozuddin Tughrai pointed out that the accusation which Iqbal was holding up, even if it were justified, would apply only to some of the poems of Hafiz. The *Divan* of Hafiz contained much else that would meet Iqbal's criterion of healthy art. The creative energies of Iqbal would be spent better if he reinterpreted Hafiz from his point of view, instead of attempting a whole scale rejection of a poet who was so close to the hearts of so many.[3] The admirers of Hafiz included, among others, Iqbal's own father, who is reported to have offered similar advice.[4]

Iqbal took the point very well. He expunged all criticism of Hafiz from the next edition of his poem, and even offered a

---

[1] The unfinished draft was later edited by the late Iqbal scholar Sabir Kalorvi and published as *Tarikh-i-Tassawwuf.*
[2] Shafique (Urdu; 2012), pp.114, 121-124
[3] Shafique (Urdu; 2012), p.219
[4] Shafique (Urdu; 2012), p.253

conditional apology.[1] In all subsequent works, he followed the advice of Qidwai, frequently quoted his favourite verses from Hafiz and even offering him a heartfelt and emotional tribute in an Urdu poem on the subject of art: 'The construction owes itself to the warmth of the blood of the architect, be it the tavern of Hafiz or the temple of Behzad'.[2]

The woman question

His views about the role of women in society were based on the principle that the inner cohesion of Muslim society depended completely on shared ideals. Inculcating these ideals in their citizens during their childhood is therefore a far more crucial need for Muslim societies, since these societies would be undone otherwise (unlike other societies that could be held together by race, country, language or economic interests).

In the time of Iqbal at least, this need of the community could best be fulfilled by mothers.[3] This was widely believed in those days in the East as well as the West. The manner in which he emphasized motherhood could appear today as if he were denying women a personality in their own right, but in the context of his own age he was only taking the moderate view and was avoiding both extremes. Britain and America had not granted women the right to vote until the 1920s, and the overall concept of women's liberation would be bitterly opposed even by a large number of enlightened Western women for a long time to come.

---

[1] Shafique (Urdu; 2012), pp.406-408
[2] Iqbal (Urdu; 1973), p.593 [or Iqbal (Urdu; 1990), p.642]. Unfortunately, a large number of reputed scholars have been misled into believing that Iqbal forever remained critical not only of Hafiz but also of all mystical and amorous poetry. This includes Schimmel (1963/1989), p.63
[3] Iqbal (1977/1995), p.134-135

On his part, Iqbal admitted frankly that there were no final answers, and the issue of women's role in society would always have to be decided afresh in view of the society's ideals as well as the spirit of the times. He was also quite clear that any legislation affecting women should meet the requirements of justice and equality. Personally, he considered divorce to be a greater evil than polygamy.[1] Still, this did not stop him from suggesting passionately that the delegation of the right of divorce to the wife, and restriction on polygamy, should be incorporated into marriage contracts.[2] In fact, through his disciple Dr. Khalifa Abdul Hakim, his influence was perhaps responsible for the incorporation of these clauses in the family laws of Pakistan. He also supported, in very clear terms, the economic rights that Islam had bestowed on women but which had been overruled by social customs.

It is difficult to say what his opinions would have been on the question of women's role in society if he were living a hundred years later. At the same time, it is hard to believe that he would have contradicted the Quaid-i-Azam ('the Great Leader') Muhammad Ali Jinnah, the chosen leader of the community who gave some very clear directions about the advancement of women after the birth of Pakistan. In the final analysis, it is quite reasonable to believe that if Iqbal was living in the present day, he would still have generally sympathetic to the opinions and practices of the average Muslims as he was in his own times, and not thrown his weight on the side of either of the two extremes.

---

[1] Iqbal (1961/2006), p.60
[2] Lecture VI, in Iqbal (1930/1934), p.161, but also emphasized in several speeches and writings, such as 'Position of Women in the East', included in Iqbal (1977/1995), pp.192-193. See also Shafique (2006/2007), pp.92, 178

'Shakespeare' (1916)

Iqbal's direct participation in the mainstream of British literature occurred through his Urdu poem 'Shakespeare', submitted along with English translation for inclusion in *A Book of Homage to Shakespeare* (1916). The book was edited by Israel Gollancz and published by a special committee in England in commemoration of the three hundredth anniversary of the Bard's death. Comprising of fourteen lines divided into two stanzas (just like the sonnets of Shakespeare, but following a different rhyme scheme), the poem impressed upon the reader through breathtaking metaphors the well-considered view of Iqbal that Shakespeare rethinks the thought of Divine Creation.[1]

The poem, along with a new translation in English, is now displayed in the café inside the compound of Shakespeare's Birthplace Museum. Its last two lines have been considered by some to be the highest praise ever bestowed upon the Bard:

> Nature guards its mysteries so jealously,
> It shall never again create one who knows so many
> secrets.[2]

The lead given by Iqbal, if followed to the end, can result in the birth of a new school of Shakespearean criticism, some fruits of which could be (a) a placement of Shakespeare in the world of the Quran; (b) the discovery of common strands in the creative geniuses of Shakespeare and such Persian poets as Nezami Ganjavi, Fariduddin Attar and Jalaluddin Rumi; (c) the similar and complementary roles of these poets in the birth of modern civilization.[3] Such researches may also reveal an extraordinary

---

[1] The phrase is taken from his private notebook; see Iqbal (1961/2006), p.130
[2] Iqbal (Urdu; 1973), p.251 [or Iqbal (Urdu; 1990), p.280]
[3] Iqbal Academy Pakistan has contributed two publications to this end in the recent years: *Shakespeare According to Iqbal* (2010) by Khurram Ali Shafique

connection between the ideas of Iqbal and his contemporary
Urdu playwright Agha Hashar Kashmiri (widely known as 'the
Indian Shakespeare' in those days), which remains one of the
most neglected areas in Iqbal Studies.[1]

The mind of Europe

'Secrets of the Self' got translated by the renowned Orientalist
and Iqbal's former teacher at Cambridge, R. A. Nicholson, and
was published from England in 1920. It got mentioned twice in
Times Literary Supplement,[2] apart from being reviewed in other
papers and journals by eminent writers including Lowes
Dickinson and E. M. Forester. The latter, whose *Passage to
India* was still in the making, observed that Iqbal has acquired
his legendary status among his people without any patronage
from the government and without receiving any international
literary award, such as the Nobel Prize.[3] Critic Herbert Read
applauded the poem in his article 'Readers and Writers' in the
journal *New Age.*[4]

Especially in England, the poem created some outrage and
started two controversies that were going to plague Iqbal Studies
for a long time and distract some of the best minds of the future
generations. They were related to (a) the European image of a
'blood-thirsty Islam'; and (b) the question of influences.

---

and *Shakespeare and Nezami* (2013) by Dr. Mahmoud Daram and Marziyeh S.
Ghoreishi.
[1] For some groundwork in this area, see Shafique (Urdu; 2010), pp. 145-152,
225-231, 279-283, 463-470, 488-491 and Shafique (Urdu; 2012), pp.159-166,
363-364, 368-373, 669-670, 805
[2] Shafique (Urdu; 2012), p.604
[3] 'Iqbal has won his vast kingdom without help from the West ...' quoted in Dr.
Riffat Hasan (1977), p.279
[4] Sir Herbert Read (1921)

The fear of a blood-thirsty Islam

The translator introduced Iqbal as 'a religious enthusiast, inspired by the vision of a New Mecca, a world-wide, theocratic, Utopian state in which all Muslims ... shall be one. He will have nothing to do with nationalism and imperialism ... It must be observed that when he speaks of religion he always means Islam. Non-Muslims are simply unbelievers, and (in theory, at any rate) the *Jihad* is justifiable, provided that it is waged "for God's sake alone"'.

Lowes Dickinson, an acquaintance of the poet from his Cambridge days and one of the architects of the League of Nations, took lead from this. 'Quite clearly Mr. Iqbal desires and looks forward to a Holy War, and that too a war of arms', he wrote in *The Nation,* London. It seems that the poem had reminded Dickinson of the bleak prophecy made recently by the Irish poet W.B. Yeats in 'The Second Coming', to which Dickinson probably alluded in the concluding paragraph:

> ... some wistful Westerners, hopeless of their own countrymen, are turning once more to look for a star in the East. What do they find? Not the star of Bethlehem, but this blood-red planet. If this book be prophetic, the last hope seems taken away.[1]

Iqbal attributed Dickinson's fears to 'the old European idea of a blood-thirsty Islam' and replied, 'Mr. Dickinson ... is quite right when he says that war is destructive, whether it is waged in the interest of Truth and Justice, or in the interests of conquest and exploitation. It must be put an end to in any case. We have seen, however, that Treaties, Leagues, Arbitrations and Conferences cannot put an end to it. Even if we secure these in a more effective manner than before, ambitious nations will substitute

---

[1] Dr. Riffat Hasan (1977), p.290

more peaceful forms of the exploitation of races supposed to be less favoured or less civilized. The truth is that we stand in need of a living personality to solve our social problems, to settle our disputes, and to place international morality on a sure basis...'[1] He accepted the possibility that 'new forces hitherto unknown' might be discovered for securing the stability of humankind, and may replace such factors as war, but he believed such time to be very distant: 'I am afraid mankind will not for a very long time to come, learn the lesson that the Great European War has taught them.'[2] History was going to prove him right in less than twenty years.

The question of influences

The translator had also given the impression that Iqbal was heavily influenced by Nietzsche. Forster picked it up in his characteristically effective style: 'The significance of Iqbal is not that he holds [the doctrine of Nietzsche] but that he manages to connect it with the Koran. Two modifications, and only two, have to be made...'[3]

Iqbal had to point out that Forster had failed to rightly understand his idea of the Perfect Man, 'which he confounds with the German thinker's Superman'. Referring to his thesis on Al-Jili (1900), he added: 'I wrote on the Sufi doctrine of the Perfect Man more than twenty years ago, long before I had read or heard anything of Nietzsche'.[4]

Back home, the majority of Muslim writers refuted the European perception of Iqbal. From the ultra-liberal M.D. Taseer to the renowned religious scholar Maulana Syed

---

[1] B. A. Dar, Ed. (1978), p.142
[2] B. A. Dar, Ed. (1978), p.144
[3] Dr. Riffat Hasan (1977), p.283
[4] B. A. Dar, Ed. (1978), p.141

Sulaiman Nadvi, the most representative writers of Muslim India were unanimous in affirming that Iqbal's philosophy was inspired by the Quran, and that it presented an enlightened vision of Islam. In an excellently written article published in Urdu in 1922, Waheed Ahmad Masud Badayuni argued that British intelligentsia was driven by a desperate desire to keep its intellectual priesthood, and had political motives in claiming that Iqbal's ideas were borrowed from the West.[1]

Muhammad Ali Jauhar

The leader who had emerged to command the undivided respect of Iqbal's community by this time, and who would soon become the best-loved contemporary throughout the Muslim world, was Muhammad Ali (1878-1931), better remembered more by his pen name, Jauhar (literally meaning 'the essence').

He had been a favoured pupil of both Sir Syed Ahmad Khan and Maulana Shibili Numani, and was among the founding members of the All-India Muslim League in December 1906. He started two newspapers soon afterwards, *Hamdard* in Urdu and *Comrade* in English. The latter became widely read even among the ruling British elite, and the editor was soon acknowledged as one of the best prose writers who ever wrote in English. Also, he was perhaps the first prominent Muslim to declare openly that he had learnt Islam from Iqbal rather than from any religious teacher, and that he followed religion as preached by Iqbal. He did not recount from this assertion even during his temporary fall-out with Iqbal in the mid-1920s.

He got into trouble with the colonial authorities soon after the outbreak of the First World War in 1914, over his leading

---

[1] The article of Badayuni is included in Shafique (Urdu; 2012), pp.845-851

article, 'The Choice of the Turks'. He and his elder brother
Shaukat Ali (collectively called 'the Ali Brothers') were placed
under detention although no charges were ever brought out
against them in public. Their prolonged detention, which
continued till 1919, raised outcry across British India.
Muhammad Ali Jinnah, widely known as 'the Ambassador of
Hindu-Muslim Unity' at that time, raised questions in the
Viceroy's Legislative Council about the detention of the Ali
Brothers.[1] Mohandas Karamchand Gandhi, having returned
home only in 1915 after spending nearly all his grown-up life in
South Africa, courted popular support in British India by
singling out the Ali Brothers 'as his first great national cause in
opposition to the British Raj'.[2]

Subsequent to their release in 1919, the Ali Brothers
became simultaneously active in the All-India Muslim League
and the Indian National Congress. This had become possible
after the Lucknow Pact of 1916, whereby the Congress had
conceded to the core demand of the League for separate
electorates.

Saving the Muslim world from the injustice of the Treaty of
Versailles was the cause the Ali Brothers were going to
champion for the next few years, at one point even risking the
gallows. The treaty had been signed in France on June 28, 1919,
and the terms imposed on the defeated nations were generally
regarded as too harsh even by impartial observers. The Muslims
of British India were especially outraged because in order to
enlist their services for the army, the British rulers had promised
explicitly that the sovereignty of the Ottoman Turkey and the
Middle East would not be compromised. Both regions were
being placed under foreign rule by the Treaty of Versailles, and
Britain was a signatory.

---

[1] Stanley Wolpert (1989), p.52
[2] Stanley Wolpert (1989), p.52

The Ali Brothers came up with three demands, widely supported by the Hindus as well as the Muslims in British India:

1. *The Arabian Peninsula and the adjoining regions of the Middle East up to Mesopotamia* should remain under Muslim rule, and the proposed state of Israel should not be established. The Ali Brothers maintained that the Muslims were religiously obliged to be in control of that region according to an explicit instruction given by the Holy Prophet (peace be upon him).

2. *The Ottoman Caliph, as the ceremonial leader of the entire Sunni sect of Islam,* should be left with sufficient temporal power for protecting the abovementioned lands, and his stature should not be reduced to a powerless spiritual leader like the Christian Pope, as had been proposed in the Treaty of Versailles.

3. *Turkey* should not be placed under the occupation of foreign powers – Greece and Italy – as had been advised by the infamous Treaty.

The Ali Brothers visited Europe for enlisting support from the liberal intelligentsia as well as to meet the Prime Minister Lloyd George. The mission failed, and had already been criticized by Iqbal in a poem 'The Beggar of Caliphate'.[1] The Ali Brothers advised their Muslim followers in British India to join the movement of 'Civil Disobedience' that was being launched by Gandhi on August 20, 1920, with the aim of securing dominion status for India. This was because Gandhi had explicitly pledged support to the three demands of the Ali Brothers – the 'Khilafat Movement', as it was called by the Muslim press.

Iqbal supported the aims of the Khilafat Movement but believed that non-cooperation could affect the economic life of the Muslim community, and therefore it required a consensus of

Muslim religious scholars from all schools of thought, including the Shia, with due facilitation to be provided by professional lawyers and economists.[2]

The leaders of the Khilafat Movement, including Jauhar, agreed in principle but believed that the requirement had already been met since rulings had been obtained from several religious scholars in favor of non-cooperation. Iqbal considered those rulings insufficient as they had been given in individual capacities. This was the beginning of a fall-out between Iqbal and the Ali Brothers, which ended only after the publication of the Nehru Report in 1928. Then Jauhar revised his position with his characteristic frankness and joined hands with Iqbal in consolidating Muslim public opinion along the lines suggested by the poet-philosopher.

Unfortunately, Jauhar died soon afterwards on January 5, 1931 – just a few days after declaring in London that he would prefer to die on the free soil of Britain unless the British granted freedom to his homeland. He was perhaps the first celebrity in the history of Islam whose death was mourned simultaneously throughout the Muslims world – thanks to modern means of communication, which had not been available in the previous centuries. He was buried in Jerusalem, in recognition of his efforts for guarding the freedom of that city. Iqbal wrote an outstanding elegy for him in Persian. The most fitting verses about Jauhar's death had been written, however, by Jauhar himself quite prophetically many years earlier: 'The whole world envies Jauhar for his death. This is granted by the Almighty, to whomever He is pleased to'.[3]

---

[1] Iqbal (Urdu; 1973), p. 254 [or Iqbal (Urdu; 1990), p.281]

[2] Shafique (Urdu; 2012), pp.596-597, 833-838

[3] بے رشک ایک خلق کو جوہر کی موت پر

یہ اُس کی دین ہے جسے پروردگار دے

'Khizr of the Way'

The charisma of Muhammad Ali Jauhar was partially because he personified the anxiety felt by Muslims all over the world after the Great European War. For the Urdu speaking world, the same discontent was captured by Iqbal in a landmark poem, 'Khizr of the Way'. It was recited by him on April 16, 1922, at the annual fundraising event of Anjuman Himayat-i-Islam, Lahore.[1]

The genesis of the poem can be traced back to a letter written by Iqbal to his friend, the Persian poet Sheikh Ghulam Qadir Girami, on July 1, 1917. In it, Iqbal mentioned his belief that the Quran sheds light on the future history of Muslims, but the special insight required for seeing this is rare and has been granted to Iqbal. He also expressed his firm resolved to write down a history of the future as third part of *Secrets and Mysteries*.[2] Discarding the earlier approaches to the Quran that had relied heavily on Greek thought, and by applying inductive reasoning, he had discovered instances of 'specific historical generalization' in the Quran. This made possible for him 'a scientific treatment of the life of human societies regarded as organisms').[3] The proposed history of the future may have evolved into *Javid Nama* (1932), but some predictions also found way in 'Khizr of the Way'.[4]

The poem comprises of a dialogue between the poet and Khizr, a legendary guide in classical Muslim literature, who is said to have found the Water of Life and hence has been living forever. He is also believed to be the 'servant of God' mentioned

---

[1] Shafique (Urdu; 2012), p.727
[2] Shafique (Urdu; 2012), p.310
[3] Lecture V in Iqbal (1930/1934), p.132. He later said in a Persian poem: 'As I washed the corrilium of Razi from my eyes, I saw destinies of the nations concealed in the Holy Book' [Iqbal (Persian; 1973), p.630].
[4] The Urdu poem appears in Iqbal (Urdu; 1973), p.255-266 [or Iqbal (Urdu; 1990), p.283-296]

in Chapter 18 of the Quran, who received knowledge from the Divine Presence, and could foresee destinies.

The poet asks five questions to Khizr, respectively related to: (a) Khizr's preference for deserts instead of cities; (b) Life; (c) imperialism; (d) Russian revolution; and (e) the Muslim World. Khizr's answers to the first two questions comprise of a quick recap of the philosophy expounded by Iqbal in *Secrets and Mysteries*. In answer to the third questions, the sage criticizes the recent political reforms of the British as eyewash, and declares: 'Imperialism is the sorcery of the dominant nations'.[1]

Khizr's answer to the fourth question traces, perhaps inadvertently, a connection between the Russian Revolution and the novel, *What Is To Be Done*. 'The human nature has broken all fetters,' says Khizr, 'How long, after all, could Adam have wept for the lost paradise'?[2]

The answer to the last question contains the most moving lines, where Khizr advises the Muslims to unite: 'Muslims ought to be united for defending the Kaaba – from the banks of the Nile up to the soil of Kashghar'.[3] He also points out that Asians are yet to realize that the freedom of the East depends on the unity of Islam (an idea soon to be echoed by the Bengali visionary C. R. Das).

The poem ends on a prophecy that was going to be fulfilled before the end of the year. After lamenting the humiliation of the Muslim nations at the hand of the Western powers, Khizr goes on to quote Rumi: 'Whenever an old edifice is reconstructed, the previous construction has to be demolished first.'[4] He then goes on to say that the old world is going to be reborn, just like Phoenix rising from its ashes.[5]

---

[1] Iqbal (Urdu; 1973), p. 260 [or Iqbal (Urdu; 1990), p.289]
[2] Iqbal (Urdu; 1990), p.293
[3] Iqbal (Urdu; 1990), p.295
[4] Iqbal (Urdu; 1990), p.294
[5] Iqbal (Urdu; 1973), p. 266 [or Iqbal (Urdu; 1990), p.296]

On September 9, less than six months after the first recital of the poem, the resistance army of Mustafa Kemal Pasha wrested Smyrna from the hands of the Allied Powers who had occupied Turkey.[1] Throughout the East, the victory was celebrated as the turning of the tables against Western imperialism, and the beginning of a new era.[2]

The time of unveiling

These signs of the time were also reflected in the attempt made by the friends of Iqbal – Sikhs and Muslims – to present him before the Western audience from the perspective of the East, and to dispel some of the myths woven around him by the Western critics. 'To unveil his charming personality to the gaze of Europe and America' was stated as the purpose of the first book about him, *A Voice from the East* – a slender volume of some 42 large pages written and published by his friend Sir Nawab Zulfiqar Ali Khan in 1922. A selection of Iqbal's Urdu verses was rendered into English for inclusion in the book by the mutual friend Sirdar Umrao Singh Sher Gill.[3]

Tracing the social and literary history of the community from the decadent days of the eighteenth century to the 'Dawn of Indian Renaissance' in the second half of the nineteenth, the author placed Iqbal in his historical and social milieu. He showed that the spirit of Iqbal's thought was 'an evangel of the future' and the 'force of intellect' possessed by him had already 'initiated potential movements in the world of thought'.[4]

---

[1] Andrew Mango (1999/2000), p.344
[2] Shafique (Urdu; 2012), pp.772, 782-785, 804-805
[3] Khan (1922/1982), p.viii. Written the active involvement of Iqbal and neglected by later scholars, the book deserves special attention.
[4] Khan (1922/1982), p.viii

He also pointed out that the poetry of Iqbal seemed to have anticipated and reflected even those universal trends that were now taking place outside his circle of influence. The author related the premonitions expressed in 'March 1907' to the current affairs of the world:

Whether it is Ireland, Egypt, India, Persia or Russia, the people there have torn the mask from their faces and are clamouring for their rights', he wrote, 'History does not relate the existence of any previous age of such a colossal revolt against organized government.[1]

Mary Parker Follett and C. R. Das

In sync with the current of Iqbal's thought was also the idea of 'new democracy', highlighted by such political thinkers as the American pioneer of management sciences, Mary Parker Follett and the great Bengali visionary Chittaranjan Das (C. R. Das).

Follett denounced Western democracy as 'old democracy', which sustained itself through a dichotomy between the government and the opposition. Discarding also the totalitarian models advocated by the Bolsheviks, she introduced the idea of a 'new democracy' based on the notion of consensus, with the aim of developing the personality of the individual. Her book, *The New State* (1918), was a detailed elaboration of the concept that was so much in line with the philosophy of Iqbal.

The Bengali visionary leader Das picked up the idea in his presidential address to the annual session of the Indian National Congress in Gaya on December 26, 1922, and cited excerpts from *The New State*.[2] He modified them for developing a holistic model for India where:

----

[1] Khan (1922/1982), p.12
[2] C. R. Das (1922), pp.43-44

a. ideas should move upward from the grass root;
b. communities should continue to evolve their own distinct characters, and yet strengthen the spiritual unity of India;
c. India should actively seek the unity of the Muslim world as part of a broader vision for the unity of the entire Asia; and
d. the ultimate aim of all political activity should be the development of a healthy personality in the individuals.[1]

A few days later, Iqbal wrote to a young Muslim journalist that Das had 'presented the same spiritual principle in a political manner' that Iqbal had presented in *Secrets and Mysteries.*[2]

Knighthood

By this time, Iqbal had also received knighthood in recognition of his literary stature, and it was announced on January 1, 1923. Thereafter, he printed his name on his stationery as Dr. Sir Muhammad Iqbal.[3] The nationalist press denounced him, completely disregarding his right to remain aloof from non-cooperation movement of Gandhi. Since this was a time when the British Raj was at the height of unpopularity, Iqbal may not have *taken* a favour from the government but *given* one by accepting the title.[4]

---

[1] C. R. Das (1922), pp.34-37, 38-47
[2] It is almost certain that Iqbal also familiarized himself with the work of Follett: a quotation used by her ('When a man's eye shall be single'; see Follett [1918], p.156) was translated by Iqbal into Persian in the dialogue of the Voice of Beauty (God) in *Javid Nama*, signifying the same concept.
[3] Dr. Javid Iqbal (Urdu; 2008), pp.329-330
[4] Shafique (2006/2007), p.103

'The Dawn of Islam' (1923)

Within months of accepting knighthood, he came out with his harshest denunciation of British imperialism so far, in 'The Dawn of Islam', a long Urdu poem recited in the annual fundraising session of Anjuman Himayat-i-Islam in March 1923.[1] It remains one of the most popular poems in its language.

The very opening of the poem was a reminder that the prophecy made in 'The Khizr of the Way' had been fulfilled and the East, especially the Muslim East, had resurrected itself after centuries of death-like sleep.[2] Inspired by the victory of the Turks over the Greek occupation armies in Smyrna six months earlier, the poem outlined the role of the Muslim nation in the order of things and emphasized its importance in the overall defence of Asia (already mentioned in the previous poem and reinforced by C. R. Das in his presidential address to the annual session of Congress a few months earlier).

The poet may have drawn freely on the presidential address of Das as well as *The New State* by Mary Parker Follett. He also alluded to an extremely popular poem of that time, 'Thank You to Europe' (1913) by Agha Hashar Kashmiri. This may explain why so many of the lines from this poem have become proverbial in Urdu. 'The narcissus weeps over its blindness for thousands of years until a seer is born in the garden', is just one of many couplets that are memorized even by those who do not know that it was about Ghazi Mustafa Kemal Pasha, later known as Ataturk.

Ataturk was the hero of the poem. Although Iqbal later criticized some of his policies, Ataturk always remained a hero in his eyes. He also believed that Ataturk was a prime target of propaganda by forces working against the solidarity of Islam.

---

[1] Shafique (2007/2009), p.107
[2] Shafique (2007/2009), p.77

'The policy of isolating the Turks from the rest of the Muslim world is still in action,' he was going to say publically in 1937, 'We hear now and then that the Turks are repudiating Islam. A greater lie was never told...'[1] In a final analysis in 1936, he condoned almost all the measures taken by the founder of modern Turkey, and especially praised: (a) 'the development of a general materialist outlook'; (b) 'the abolition of ... the licentiate *ulema';* and (c) 'the abolition of the Caliphate'. Other measures, on which Iqbal did not offer his comments but still declared them to be permitted by Islam, were: (d) 'the abolition of the old dress'; (e) 'the abolition of polygamy'; and (f) separation of Church and state (which in a Muslim majority state could not mean the same thing that it did in Europe).

The only innovations of Ataturk that Iqbal considered to be errors of judgement were: (g) 'the introduction of the Latin script' and 'the recitation of the Quran in Turkish'; and (h) 'the adoption of the Swiss code with its rule of inheritance'. However, he also said that Ataturk was among those personalities about whom 'the history of nations shows that even their mistakes have sometimes borne good fruit'.[2]

Regarding the adoption of 'racial and nationalist ideals' by Turks and Persians, Iqbal described the attitude of Islam towards the problem of race as one of 'stooping to conquer without itself becoming a race-making factor', which was the only rational and workable attitude 'considering the mightiness of the problem of race and the amount of time which the deracialization of mankind must necessarily take'.[3]

---

[1] Iqbal (1977/1995), p.295
[2] Iqbal (1977/1995), p.232-236
[3] Iqbal (1977/1995), p.236-237

The Message of the East (1923/24)

The Message of the East (Payam-i-Mashriq) was the second book of Iqbal's poetry and was self-published from Lahore in May, 1923. It was in Persian and comprised of quatrains, ghazals and lyrical poems. It sold out quickly, and a revised and enlarged second edition was published the next year.[1]

As stated in the preface, the book was intended to be a friendly response to the Divan of the German poet-philosopher Goethe.[2] The book addressed three burning issues of the time: (a) the decline of the West; (b) the rise of the East; and (c) possibilities for the future.

The decline of the West had been admitted by others as well. According to the German historian Oswald Spengler, every civilization had a fixed period, and the modern Western civilization was near its end.[3] According to the British writer H.G. Wells (often called 'the historian of the future'), this decline was universal, and was due to the collapse of some traditional society that, according to him, had existed before the birth of modern civilization.[4]

Overlaps between these worldviews and Iqbal's are so many that they often eclipse the points of departure. In The Message of the East, he had actually offered an alternative point of view. Its highlights were:

---

[1] Now included in Iqbal (Persian; 1973), pp.171-392. For publication history, see Shafique (2006/2007), p.108 and Hashmi (Urdu; 1982/2010), pp.148-150.

[2] Iqbal (Persian; 1973), p.177. For a comparative study of Goethe and Iqbal, see Goethe, Iqbal and the Orient by M. Ikram Chaghatai (1999), which is also useful as an introduction to the vast corpus of writings on the subject.

[3] 'The future of the West is ... strictly limited and defined as to form and duration ...' Oswald Spengler (1926/1927), p.39

[4] 'The old civilizations created tradition, and lived by tradition. To-day the power of tradition is destroyed. The body of our state is civilization still, but its spirit is the .spirit of the nomadic world.' H. G. Wells (1920/1921), p.1097

a. geographical basis of nationality had been falsified by the Great European War (later named World War I);
b. European politicians were too conservative to find an alternative basis for nationalism consistent with the spirit of time;
c. devastation caused by the Great War had generally resulted in 'debilitation of the vital forces' in European society;
d. for these reasons, European society had now become incapable of discovering a healthy literary ideal that could give it a new direction; and
e. Europe was likely to become 'Magian' in spirit.

He singled out America as an exception, a 'healthy element' in Western civilization because it was free from the trammels of tradition, and its collective intuition was capable of receiving inspiration from the spirit of modern times.

Among contemporary European thinkers, he singled out two whose writings could offer a glimpse into the shape of things to come: the French thinker Henri Bergson and the German genius Albert Einstein. The great point of similarity between Iqbal and Bergson was that both considered evolution to be creative, in which the will to live a higher and fuller life plays an important role. The subtle differences between their points of view have been summarized by a modern writer in the following terms:

> Iqbal considers the creative will as thoughtful and intelligent, and evolution purposive, whereas to Bergson it is a blind and non-teleological force. Again, Bergson takes human personalities as mere shadows of the 'Elan' [the will to live], whereas Iqbal states that human egos are real by themselves. Further, to Bergson duration is prior to the self, but to Iqbal there

can be no conception of duration without a self, i.e.,
self or ego is prior to time and space.[1]

While the literature and ideas of Europe had facilitated the
reawakening of the East up to this point, Iqbal foresaw that the
future poets, philosophers, saints and statesmen in Europe were
likely to be inspired by decadence, whose sole ministry would
be 'to glorify, by the force of a seductive art of logic, all that is
ignoble and ugly in the life of their people.'[2] The rising East
should fortify itself mentally against such European apostles
who would unconsciously clothe despair in the glittering
garment of hope. To this end, Iqbal asked the nations of the East,
especially the Muslim East, to remember that the new world that
they wanted to bring to reality had to be formed first in the realm
of imagination, and in the depths of their souls.[3]

The 'time of unveiling' prophesied by him had arrived. He
now foretold that a great change was around the corner, so
positive in its spiritual and cultural aspects that 'what should not
have been but was, will not be anymore; and what was not but
should have been, will be'.[4]

The book offered a few glimpses of this revolution. To
depict Rumi and Goethe discussing *Faust* in heaven was a
unique idea at that time.[5] Yet, the allegory has partially been
realized today when Rumi is being named as the most popular
poet in America, and Shakespeare is part of the emotional
baggage of the East (arguably even more than the West).

---

[1] Qaiser (2012), p.146
[2] Iqbal (1977/1995), pp.227-228
[3] Iqbal (Persian; 1973), pp.182
[4] Iqbal (Persian; 1973), p.192
[5] Sometime later, it intrigued a young German woman so much that she
embarked on a lifelong study of Iqbal and later became renowned as
Annemarie Schimmel.

The young East

These ideas became the inspiration for a fourth generation of writers in the Islamic Movement of literature, which had passed through Hali, Akbar and Iqbal. The new generation comprised of a large number of Indian Muslim writers who made their debut between the beginning of the First World War in 1914 and the end of British rule in 1947. They included Mian Basheer Ahmad, Hafeez Jallundhri, Mian M. Aslam, Tufail Hoshiarpuri, Waheed Ahmad Masud Badayuni, Aslam Jairajpuir, Naseer Ahmad Nasir, Syed Nazeer Niazi, Shakeel Badayuni, Raghib Muradabadi, and a host of others who followed the general trends of the movement and reflected the basic spirit of Iqbal's message as embodied in *Secrets and Mysteries*.

Appearing in the wake of a larger than life poet-philosopher, the new writers ensured freshness by picking up amusing subjects, entertaining themes and simple expression. Discovering folds of meaning in this type of text relied purely on the 'will' of the audience.[1] The pioneer of this new style was Hafeez Jallandhri, whose phenomenally popular poem, 'Still I Am Young', ('Abhi Tou Mien Jawan Hoon'), came to define the 'Roaring 20s' for the Urdu speaking East (including non-Muslims). It emanated a pagan ethos, hedonistically celebrating the pleasures of the world, as seen through youthful eyes. Superficially, it could be seen as a contrast to the predominantly Islamic sobriety of Iqbal but it was actually a loud and clear affirmation of his statement, 'The East, and especially the Muslim East, has opened its eyes after a centuries-long slumber'.[1]

In retrospect, the poem can be revisited as a song of defiance and resistance against the decadent Europe, which was

---

[1] Hence it may not be possible to agree with the assumption that 'one cannot speak of an Iqbalian poetical tradition' (Mir (2006), p.56.

trying to impose on the rising East a culture of senility, pessimism and high seriousness (respectively symbolized by T. S. Eliot, W.B. Yeats and James Joyce, along with others). Europe may or may not have had a reason to feel pessimistic after World War I, but the East certainly had no reason to do so. By celebrating life innocently and joyfully, and through their sheer optimism, the new writers of the Islamic Movement saved the national mind from giving in to the pessimistic influence of contemporary European literature. Thus they ensured 'orderly transmission of collective experience'.[2]

Consciously or unconsciously, they facilitated the development of 'the austere type' of character that had been identified by Iqbal as the important need of the community (and which the community was demanding, even regardless of Iqbal). The convivial type of character represented in the early poetry of Hafeez (such as 'Abhi Tou Mien Jawan Hoon') also evolved gradually into the austere type through the later poetry, which included such masterpieces as *The Grand Epic of Islam* (Shahnama-i-Islam), a hymn of Krishna that was sung at one time by worshippers in Banaras, and the official national anthem of the state that was said to be the brainchild of Iqbal.

An exceptionally larger than life personality from this generation was Hakim Ahmed Shuja. He was one of the most special disciples of Iqbal and co-edited a series of textbooks with him. He was a poet, educationist, playwright, screenwriter, novelist, literary critic, social historian, amateur philosopher and a commentator of the Quran. As a dramatist, he was the pioneer of detective fiction in Urdu, since a stage play written by him was the first original detective story in that language. As a screenwriter, and with the help of his filmmaker son Anwar Kemal Pasha, he became one of the pioneers of the new film

---

[1] Preface to *The Message of the East* (1923) in Iqbal (Persian; 1973).
[2] The quote is from Iqbal (1997/1995), p.130

industry in Pakistan, soon after the creation of the state. As a commentator of the Quran, he offered a non-sectarian approach that eventually led to the pioneering work of his granddaughter Dr. Riffat Hasan in the field of Muslim feminism. The Islamic Movement of Modern Literature was to go a long way.

Textbooks

The textbooks that Shuja co-edited with Iqbal were titled *Urdu Course,* and comprised of four books, respectively for Grades 5, 6, 7 and 8. The books for the three latter grades were published in 1924. The book for Grade 5 was added in 1928.[1] They remained the approved textbooks for use in Punjab, the United Province (UP) and Madras for a long time, and were subsequently used in Pakistan until the early 1950s.[2]

Shuja also contributed a one-act play, 'The Clever Detective' (Hoshiyar Suraghrisan), for one of the books. It was perhaps the earliest detective story in Urdu (with the partial exception of a novel ascribed to Agha Hashar Kashmiri, said to have been published in 1902).[3]

Iqbal also compiled a textbook of Persian, *The Mirror of Ajam* (Aina-i-Ajam), for Grade 10. Apart from classics, it also included masterpieces by living authors such as Mahmood Tarzi of Afghanistan and Sayyed Muhammad-Ali Jamalzadeh of Persia.[4]

---

[1] An excellent history of the publication of this series is given by Hashmi (Urdu; 1982/2010), pp.411-417

[2] A new edition, thoroughly revised and updated by the present author for contemporary classrooms, is now being brought out by Topline Publishers under the supervision of Iqbal Academy Pakistan.

[3] The possible influence of Iqbal on the subsequent development of detective fiction in Urdu is discussed in the Urdu trilogy by the present author: *Psycho Mansion* (2011), *Rana Palace* (2011) and *Danish Manzil* (forthcoming).

[4] Hashmi (Urdu; 1982/2010), pp.417-419. In 1913, he permitted his name to be ascribed to a textbook of history, *Tarikh-i-Hind,* with disastrous results. The

The Call of the Marching Bell (1924)

Around the same time as the first three textbooks co-edited with Shuja, the third book of Iqbal's poetry also appeared on the scene. It was the long-awaited volume of Urdu poems, self-published from Lahore in September 1924.[1] It was aptly titled *The Call of the Marching Bell* (Baang-i-Dara), an expression used more than once in the poems included between the covers.

Poems were presented in an approximately chronological order and were divided into three sections: Part 1, up to 1905; Part 2, from 1905 to 1908 (the years when the poet was a student in Europe); and Part 3, since 1908.

Explanatory notes, which accompanied some of the early poems when they were first published in *Makhzan,* were omitted now. The most fateful of such omissions pertained to 'The Sun' – Iqbal's translation of 'Gayetri', a widely recited hymn from the sacred texts of Hinduism. The poem addressed the Sun as *'parvardigar'*, a Persian expression literally meaning 'the sustainer', but conventionally reserved for God, and it ended on the prayer: 'O Sun! Grant us the ray of awareness, and illuminate our intellect with the light of the heart'.[2] In the prefatory note that had appeared with the poem in *Makhzan* in 1902, Iqbal had explained that the Sun metaphorically addressed in the poem was an allusion to the Divine Illumination from which the celestial body received its light.[3] Omitting this note from *The Call of the Marching Bell,* Iqbal captioned the poem as

---

book, apparently produced without his active involvement, turned out to be pejorative about some Muslim heroes and politically incorrect in some other ways. See Hashmi (Urdu; 1982/2010), pp.419-428.
[1] Now included in Iqbal (Urdu; 1973), pp.1-292 [or Iqbal (Urdu; 1990), pp.17-324]. For publication history, see Shafique (2006/2007), p.109 and Hashmi (Urdu; 1982/2010), pp.52-58
[2] Iqbal (Urdu; 1973), p.43 [or Iqbal (Urdu; 1990), p.75].
[3] Shafique (Urdu; 2009), p.235

'Translation of Gayetri', perhaps presuming that the readers would find it self-evident that the translation of a Vedic hymn by a Muslim poet is to be taken as a literary exercise, not necessarily meaning that the poet shares the beliefs expressed in it. This implication, if intended by him, was lost on the cleric of the second largest mosque in Lahore, who issued a formal denunciation against the poet within a year of the publication of the book.[1]

On the whole, the book presented an impressionistic biography of the poet's mind. It was possible to trace his emotional and intellectual evolution through a careful study of the volume. There was a thematic relationship between poems, implied in their sequencing, which created a kind of a subtext.[2]

Imperium in imperio[3]

'In a collection of Dr. Iqbal's Urdu poetry just published at Lahore, his poems are divided into three periods', it was observed about *The Call of the Marching Bell* in an article published in *The Tribune* on December 10, 1924. The author complained that poems belonging to the third period were 'full of sectarian religionism'. The article was part of a series collectively titled 'The Hindu-Muslim Problem', and written by the enigmatic nationalist leader, Lala Lajpat Rai. In addition to giving thirteen commandments to the Indian Muslims, he also contributed an idea that would have a far-reaching impact: partitions in India along religious lines.

---

[1] Dr. Javid Iqbal (Urdu; 2008), pp.351-353
[2] See Shafique (2007/2009), pp.61-84
[3] Meaning 'an empire within an empire' (or 'a state within a state'), the expression was used by Iqbal in an oral comment during his presidential address to the annual session of the All-India Muslim League in Allahabad in 1930.

Partition, and partitions

In his series of articles, Rai proposed 'a clear partition of India into a Muslim India and a non-Muslim India'.

He was enigmatic. He espoused the secularism proposed by the Congress but also lent support to Hindu Mahasabha, which was founded in 1914 in order to campaign for (a) Hindu political unity; (b) rejection of the Muslim demand for separate electorates; and (c) reconversion of Muslims to Hinduism (carried out through an offshoot movement separately known as Shuddhi).[1] Best remembered by posterity as the party to which the assassins of Gandhi belonged and that later gave birth to the Bharatiya Janta Party, the Mahasabha was a rising power in the early 1920s. Iqbal considered it to be 'the real representative of the Hindu masses' as compared to the Congress.[2]

The period 1916 to 1923 marked the best seven years for Hindu-Muslim unity, perhaps in the entire history of India. It started when the Congress accepted the Muslim demand for separate electorates, considered to be the key to the unity of India by such confirmed nationalists as Sir Pherozeshah Mehta, Gopal Krishna Gokhale and C. R. Das. In 1923, the increased popularity of the Mahasabha, with its opposition of separate electorates, coincided with an unprecedented wave of Hindu-Muslim riots, putting an end to the short-lived period of unity (and the riots would continue till the end of British rule in 1947).[3] Wording it rather like a threat, Rai suggested in his articles in 1924 that partition was the only solution acceptable to Hindus if Muslims did not give up separate electorates:

---

[1] S. K. Mittal and Irfan Habib (1979), p.21

[2] Iqbal (1943/2001), p.

[3] By July 1927, Iqbal was publicly stating, 'We are actually living in a state of civil war'. See Iqbal (1977/1995), p.57

My suggestion is that the Punjab should be partitioned into two provinces, the Western Punjab with a large Muslim majority, to be a Muslim-governed Province; and the Eastern Punjab, with a large Hindu-Sikhs majority, to be a non-Muslim-governed Province ... I will make the same suggestion [for Bengal] ...

Under my scheme the Muslims will have four Muslim States: (1) The Pathan Province or the North-West Frontier, (2) Western Punjab, (3) Sindh, and (4) Eastern Bengal. If there are compact Muslim communities in any other part of India, sufficiently large to form a Province, they should be similarly constituted. But it should be distinctly understood that this is not a united India. It means a clear partition of India into a Muslim India and a non-Muslim India.

Since the Indian subcontinent had comprised of autonomous states when the British took it, the suggestion of readjustment between units was not new. Poet and activist Maualana Hasrat Mohani had suggested it as recently as in his presidential address at the annual session of the All-India Muslim League in December 1921 (and Rai mentioned this in his articles).

Rai's original contribution to the discourse comprised of the suggestions that Punjab and Bengal should also be partitioned, and the populations of Hindus and Muslims should be transferred on a massive scale.[1]

---

[1] These two disastrous elements were not included in Iqbal's proposal of 1930 or the Muslim demand for Pakistan later on. In April 1947, the Viceroy Lord Mountbatten asked Jinnah about 'Bengal united at the price of its remaining out of Pakistan'. Jinnah replied, without hesitation, 'I should be delighted. What is the use of Bengal without Calcutta; they had much better remain united and independent; I am sure that they would be on friendly terms with us.' See record of interview held on April 26, 1947. N. Mansergh and E.W.R. Lumby (Ed.)., *Transfer of Power,* vol. X, 452-453; quoted in Wolpert (1984/1989), p.322. Wolpert thinks that 'Jinnah would have welcomed the emergence of an

Rai is said to have retracted from his statement later,[1] but then his whole attitude towards Muslims, and that of the communal Hindus, had been something like, 'I hate you—Don't leave me'.[2] It can hardly be called a coincidence that twenty-three years later, just after the Muslims of India had voted for an independent state envisioned in the light of Iqbal's message and Jinnah's idealism, the Congress revived both the suggestions of Rai (i.e. the partitions of Punjab and Bengal, and mass migrations), and forced them on the Muslims.[3] The attendant evils of 'hate, suspicion, and resentment' followed.[4]

The Bengal Pact

Rai's suggestion in 1924, that the province of Bengal should be partitioned, was an about-turn in the history of Indian nationalism.

In the census of 1921, the Muslim population in Bengal had overtaken the Hindu population, and had become a Muslim majority province – unlike 1905, when it was a Hindu majority province, and the communal Hindus as well as the Congress had opposed its partition. If it were now to be partitioned into two provinces, Hindus would gain majority in one of them. The prosperous city of Calcutta, which was the hub of the economic life of Bengal, would fall in the Hindu province and the Muslim

---

independent, united Bengal with open arms; but Nehru and Patel considered it an anathema to Congress and Indian interests...' (p.320)

[1] Dr. Javid Iqbal (Urdu; 2008), p.452
[2] Allusion to the title of a book by Kreisman and Strau (2010). Iqbal had said that Gandhi's message to the Untouchables amounted to this: 'Do not leave Hinduism. Remain in it without being part of it.' See Iqbal (1977/1995), p.289
[3] The League accepted partition with the disclaimer that although its Council 'cannot agree to the partition of Bengal and the Punjab, or give its consent to such partition, it has to consider HMG [His Majesty's Government]'s plan for the transfer of power as a whole...' See Ahmad (2006), p.325
[4] The quote is taken from Lecture VII in Iqbal (1930/1934), p.178

province could be left without sufficient means for sustaining itself.

The changed situation of Bengal had already been addressed by C. R. Das. In December 1923, he had reached an agreement with prominent Muslims leaders in the province, incorporating practically all the demands of the Muslims. Flanked by ardent young disciples, such as Huseyn Shaheed Suhrawardy and Subhas Chandrabose, he got the Bengal Pact ratified by the councillors of his newly founded Swarajist Party on December 16, 1923, and by the Bengal Provincial Congress Committee two days later. In the wake of outcry from the Hindu community and its press, the Pact was rejected in the annual session of the Congress held at Cocanada later that month. Das did not give up and got it ratified by the Bengal Provincial Congress Conference held at Sirajganj in June 1924. Unfortunately, it was repudiated soon after his untimely death on June 16, 1925.[1]

The election of 1926

The Muslim demand for separate electorates had been conceded by the British Government in 1919. However, the first two elections held under the new reforms, respectively in 1920 and 1923, were boycotted by the Congress and the turnout had remained so poor that it could not be called the general will of the people. Thus the election of 1926 became the occasion when the Indian Muslims finally exercised their right of communal representation in a general election with substantial turnout. The goal adopted twenty years earlier was achieved.

---

[1] http://www.banglapedia.org/HT/B_0412.HTM Retrieved on May 31, 2013

Once again, the turning point in the life of the community coincided with a new phase in the mental life of Iqbal. Also, just like twenty years earlier, he had premonitions about it. He had confided to a young friend two years earlier that a phase in his life that started during his stay in Europe was about to end, and some great change in his life could surprise everyone.[1]

The change came when he contested the election of 1926 for membership of the Punjab Legislative Council. He was elected as an independent candidate backed by the Khilafat Committee.[2]

To some, it came as a surprise. Perhaps the best explanation of why he decided to become a practising politician was offered by a later writer who observed that the appeal of his poetry 'was not only to the literary or the intellectual classes. He was aware of the power of poetry over the emotions of Muslim peoples at all levels ... It is as if in each willing and consenting ear the poet were whispering: "Be a hero!"' Therefore it became incumbent upon him 'to provide the conditions under which the qualities that he was invoking could find scope for their display, and the way towards which he was guiding them could find extension.'[3] This is perhaps a very good description of what Iqbal was about to do in the final phase of his career, which was about to begin in 1927.

---

[1] See the diaries of Ghulam Rasool Mehr reproduced in Alvi (1988).
[2] He was opposed by one contestant but secured a vast majority.
[3] Justice A. R. Cornelius (2004), p.97

Chapter Three
Transcendence, 1927-1946

The year 1927 marked the beginning of a new phase in the career of Iqbal, and the beginning of a new stage in the history of his nation. Both began to set their gaze on a futuristic state of their own, just as the rest of the East was throbbing with a renewed yearning for true independence. Iqbal died in 1938, but his dream was fulfilled posthumously through the combined verdict of his community in the election of 1945-46. The study of this final phase of his career should therefore focus on how he was able to achieve such immortality, i.e. the extraordinary bonding with his community due to which he became the only poet or philosopher to be credited with the birth of a nation and a state, and that too after his death.

Iqbal in politics

Beginning in 1927, he started a lifelong effort to implement through politics the vision that he had presented through literature and philosophy.

The new legislative council was inaugurated on January 23, 1927 and completed its tenure in 1930. In the council, Iqbal remained more or less isolated, so that 'his speeches ... for the well-being of the common man remained collectively a cry in the wilderness.'[1] Although he did not seek re-election, he remained active in politics in other ways forever after. He was nominated president of the All-India Muslim League in 1930, and proposed and predicted the birth of that a Muslim state 'at least' in the North-West of British India.

By the beginning of the 1930s, he 'had entered the front rank of politicians of the Muslim community'.[2] In 1932, he also became the president of the All-India Muslim Conference (set up as a joint platform for Muslim political parties during the decline of the Muslim League). He was invited to the Second Round Table Conference in London in 1931 as the president of the Muslim League, and to the Third Round Table Conference in 1932 as the president of the Muslim Conference.

His prolonged final illness, commencing in January 1934, curtailed his professional and political activities.[3] Fortunately, Jinnah had just returned on the political scene, and Iqbal happily became a follower. It seems that Jinnah, in turn, benefited from the political strategies that had been evolved by Iqbal.

The will to will the common will

Mary Parker Follett had defined the new democracy as 'the large, still larger, ever larger life', the germinating centre of which is *'the will to will the common will'*.[4] In the political career of Iqbal, we find three strategies for putting this concept into practice:

a. *Treat the general will of the community as a source of wisdom, and always refer to it as the final arbiter in disputes with other parties.* Examples: the Muslims of

---

[1] Hafeez Malik (2009), p.43
[2] Dr. Parveen Shaukat Ali (1978), p.325
[3] Dr. Javid Iqbal (Urdu; 2008), p.597
[4] Follett (1918), p.49.

British India considered separate electorates to be indispensable for their collective life (unless the political scenario changed, such as with the creation of the state proposed by Iqbal). Iqbal defended their position but also stated that if the majority of the Muslims gave up the demand, he would also give it up and work together with everyone else.[1] Those who differed from the verdict of the community were regarded by him as standing aloof from 'the general body of Muslims'.[2] Thus, he reiterated through politics his philosophical stance that universal agreement was the fundamental principle of Muslim constitutional theory.

b. *Do not start negotiating details when there is no agreement on the fundamental principle.* Examples: he applauded the Muslim delegates of the First Round Table Conference for 'pressing for a solution of the communal question before the question of responsibility in the Central Government is finally settled'.[3] He maintained the same position in the Second Round Table Conference, in which he was himself a delegate.[4]

c. *The Muslims of British India should be represented by one party only, and nobody outside that party should be speaking for them. The party itself should allow as many factions as possible, to ensure accommodation of diverse points of view.* Examples: this principle was stated clearly in his Lahore Address (see below).[5] It was

---

[1] Iqbal (1977/1995), p.269
[2] See, for instance, Iqbal (1977/1995), p.270
[3] Shafique (2006/2007), p.146
[4] Iqbal (1977/1995), p.34
[5] Iqbal (1977/1995), p.46. According to Dr. Hafeez Malik (2009), p.279, there were no less than twenty political parties, 'claiming Muslim loyalty, sometimes with diametrically opposed political programs.'

later invoked for evaluating the activities of his colleagues.

In the years after the death of Iqbal, all three political strategies became the hallmark of Muhammad Ali Jinnah, whom his followers began to see as an incarnation of the ideal hero envisioned in Iqbal's poetry – the austere type of character.

Persian Psalms (1927)

Six months after his election, Iqbal brought out the fourth book of his poetry, *Persian Psalms* (Zuboor-i-Ajam). It was in Persian, and was self-published from Lahore in June 1927.[1]

The theme was the transition of a nation from political bondage to independence, and the title alluded to the book of the prophet-king through whom the Children of Israel won their promised land.[2] The book had been started in 1924, with premonitions about the beginning of a new phase in the life of its author and of his community. It attempted to offer four things for achieving and sustaining freedom:

- An experience of one's creative relationship with God through a process of progressive change; offered through 56 sequenced poems comprising 'Part 1'[3]
- An experience of being co-worker with God in shaping and reshaping the world and its destiny; offered through 75 sequenced poems comprising 'Part 2'[4]

---

[1] Now included in Iqbal (Persian; 1973), pp.393-588. For publication history, see Shafique (2006/2007), p. 119 and Hashmi (Urdu; 1982/2010), pp.163-166
[2] The working title, mentioned by the author in English, was 'The Songs of a Modern David'. See letter written by him in July 1924 and cited in Hashmi (Urdu; 1982/2010), p.164
[3] Iqbal (Persian; 1973), pp.395-451
[4] Iqbal (Persian; 1973), pp.453-533

- A new understanding of things based on one's changed position as the citizen of a free nation; offered through a masnavi, 'The New Garden of Mystery'[1]

- An objective awareness of the characteristics that appear in fine arts, music and religion due to the psychological effects of slavery; and to know how to receive inspiration from the architectural heritage of the bygone days; this was the subject of the fourth part, a masnavi, 'The Book of Slavery'[2]

Subsequently, some of the poems gained widespread popularity in the Persian speaking world, their first lines acquiring the status of modern proverbs – such as the poet's passionate address to the youth, 'I burn like a tulip in your garden. O youth of the Persianate world, by your soul and mine!'[3]

His own comment about the book was that it should suffice the intellectual needs of the Muslims for the next hundred and fifty years. He now started calling himself a 'qalandar' – an ecstatic mystic with special powers – in his poems.[4]

'The New Garden of Mystery'

As mentioned above, the third part of the book was a long poem in Persian. The nine questions and answers that formed this poem summarized the worldview that the author had unfolded gradually over the previous twenty years. It offered a new understanding of things by redefining the following nine concepts:[5]

---

[1] Iqbal (Persian; 1973), pp.535-567
[2] Iqbal (Persian; 1973), pp.571-587
[3] Iqbal (Persian; 1973), p.517
[4] Iqbal (Persian; 1973), pp.395 is the first instance of this in his poetry.
[5] In the summary which follows, I have identified the topic of each question. Quotations used in the short answers are taken from the *Reconstruction,* but

1. THOUGHT: *First of all I am intrigued about my thought. Why it is sometimes needed, sometimes shunned?[1]*

    In its essential nature, thought is dynamic and unfolds itself like the seed which, from the very beginning, carries within itself the organic unity of the tree as a present fact. The illumination of the world thus revealed within is meant to show the way of capturing the world of matter outside. The ideal, i.e. the world within, is therefore connected with the real, i.e. the world without, and the former should be used for the conquest of the latter. What is to be avoided is a focus on just one of these, excluding the other.

2. KNOWLEDGE: *What is this ocean whose shore is knowledge? What is that pearl which is found in its depth?[2]*

    Life is the ocean, and knowledge and consciousness are among its many shores. Life (including the physical world) and our consciousness of it are integrated with each other, just as the shore and the ocean are not independent but can only be defined through each other.

    Therefore, things are not formed by causes but by ends and purposes.[3] These lie within the depths of the nature of things. Their knowledge can only be obtained from within. We can acquire such knowledge about ourselves at least, since 'my perception of my own self is internal, intimate, and profound'.[4] This 'coherent wholeness of personality'[5] is the pearl that is to be found in the depth of the ocean of life.

---

used in strict conformity with the answers given in the Persian text of the poem, which can be found in Iqbal (Persian; 1973), pp.535-567

[1] Iqbal (Persian; 1973), pp.540.

[2] Iqbal (Persian; 1973), p.543.

[3] Lecture II in Iqbal (1930/1934), pp.40-41

[4] Lecture II in Iqbal (1930/1934), p.44

[5] Lecture II in Iqbal (1930/1934), p.47

3. UNION: *What is the union of the contingent and the necessary? What are near and far, more and less?*[1]

The question becomes easier to answer if it is reworded as: 'Does the universe confront God as His "other", with space intervening between Him and it'?[2] The answer is that space, time, and matter are not independent realities but interpretations that thought puts on the free creative energy of God. Reality is, therefore, essentially spirit.

4. SEPARATION: *How did the eternal and temporal separate, that one became the world, and the other God? If the knower and known are one pure essence, what are the aspirations of this handful of dust?*[3]

God is the Ultimate Ego. From the Ultimate Ego only egos proceed. This is how the eternal and temporal got separated, but *why* is more important than *how*. The ego, in its finitude, is imperfect as a unity of life. Therefore, its nature is wholly 'aspiration after a unity more inclusive, more effective, more balanced, and unique', which may not be possible in its present form, but 'who knows how many different kinds of environment it needs for its organization as a perfect unity'?[4]

5. SELF: *What am I? Tell me what 'I' means. What is the meaning of 'travel into yourself'?*[5]

The self or ego has two sides: efficient and appreciative. On its 'efficient' side, it is the practical self of daily life in its dealing with the external order of things, which weaves a kind of veil around the other side of the self, i.e. the appreciative self. We sink into that only 'in the moments of

---

[1] Iqbal (Persian; 1973), p.546.
[2] Lecture III in Iqbal (1930/1934), p.62
[3] Iqbal (Persian; 1973), p.549.
[4] Lecture IV in Iqbal (1930/1934), p.93
[5] Iqbal (Persian; 1973), p.552.

profound meditation' (when the efficient self is in abeyance).[1] Then we reach the inner centre of experience, where the states of consciousness melt into each other; time is felt and not thought and calculated; and destiny appears revealed as 'the inward reach of a thing' actualizing itself 'without any feeling of external compulsion'.[2]

6. SELFLESSNESS: *What is that part which is greater than its whole? What is the way to find that part?*[3]

That part is the human ego. It is greater than the whole of what it sees, because it alone is capable of being conscious of itself (see answer to Q.2). The ultimate spiritual basis of all life is eternal but reveals itself in variety and change. Therefore, the ego is free from within but restricted externally.

Love is the way through which one can realize this ideal nature of one's own self. Love is capable of seeking 'a purely psychological foundation of human unity', creating fresh loyalties without any ceremonials to keep them alive, and making it possible for human being to be emancipated from the restrictions imposed by 'earth-rootedness'.[4]

7. COMPLETION: *Of what sort is this traveller who is the wayfarer? Of whom shall I say that this person has achieved completion?*[5]

The ultimate aim of the ego is not to *see* something, but to *be* something. In this effort, it develops the ambition to come into direct contact with the Ultimate Reality. One who stands unshaken in the Divine Presence is the one about whom it

---

[1] Lecture II in Iqbal (1930/1934), p.45
[2] Lecture II in Iqbal (1930/1934), p.47
[3] Iqbal (Persian; 1973), p.555.
[4] Lecture VI in Iqbal (1930/1934), p.139
[5] Iqbal (Persian; 1973), p.558.

could be said that the person has achieved completion – by acquiring a more precise definition of one's self, 'which deepens the whole being of the ego, and sharpens its will with the creative assurance that the world is not something to be merely seen or known through concepts, but something to be made and re-made by continuous action'.[1]

Still, the journey doesn't end, as life is one and continuous. Human being marches 'always onward to receive ever fresh illuminations from an Infinite Reality that "every moment appears in a new glory"'.[2]

8.   'I AM THE CREATIVE TRUTH': *What point does the claim, 'I am the Creative Truth' imply? Do you think that this mystery was mere nonsense?*[3]

In the religious life of Islam, the development of the unity of inner experience reached its culmination in the well-known words of the 10th Century mystic Mansur Hallaj, 'I am the creative truth'. The phrase seems almost a challenge flung against the philosophers and theologians who, under the influence of pre-Islamic ideas, had failed to observe that the Quran declares this experience to be one of the three sources of knowledge (along with History and Nature). The contemporaries of Hallaj as well as his successors failed to arrive at a correct interpretation of his experience, which was the realization and bold affirmation of the reality and permanence of the human ego in a profounder personality.

9.   AWARENESS: *Who was it that at last became aware of the secret of Unity? What is it that a knower of secrets comes to know at last?*[1]

---

[1] Lecture VII in Iqbal (1930/1934), p.187
[2] Lecture IV in Iqbal (1930/1934), p.117
[3] Iqbal (Persian; 1973), p.561.

The body is accumulated action of the soul, or its habit, in the physical world. Therefore, the ego can understand and master the physical world only by viewing it as a system of cause and effect. However, that is not a final expression of the nature of Reality.

The Ultimate Ego has permitted the finite ego to emerge as a free causality, capable of private initiative (and thereby the Ultimate Ego has 'limited His freedom of His own free will').[2] It is open to human being 'to belong to the meaning of the universe and become immortal' but it can only be 'as an ever-growing ego'.[3]

Six Lectures (1930)

He was obviously revisiting the first seven of the above-mentioned questions when he delivered his famous seven lectures over the next few years.[4] The first six were undertaken at the request of the Madras Muslim Association and delivered at Madras, Hyderabad, and Aligarh in 1929. They were self-published from Lahore in May 1930 as *Six Lectures on the Reconstruction of Religious Thought in Islam*.[5] (A seventh lecture was delivered in London in 1932. It was added to the revised second edition, which came out in 1934 with a shorter title, *The Reconstruction of Religious Thought in Islam*).[6]

---

[1] Iqbal (Persian; 1973), p.564.
[2] Lecture IV, Iqbal (1930/1934), p.
[3] Lecture IV, Iqbal (1930/1934), p.
[4] This is my inference.
[5] Hashmi (Urdu; 1982/2010), p.317
[6] The titles of the lectures were: (a) 'Knowledge and Religious Experience'; (b) 'The Philosophical Test of the Revelations of Religious Experience'; (c) 'The Conception of God and the Meaning of Prayer'; (d) 'The Human Ego – His Freedom and Immortality'; (e) 'The Spirit of Muslim Culture'; (f) 'The

The stage of concrete thought

He proposed that religion, philosophy and higher poetry could complement each other in a common quest if the subject matter was approached with a will, and not just as a matter of intellect or understanding.[1] The underlying assumption was that humanity was perpetually evolving, and history could be divided into three broad phases: (a) period of minority; (b) the birth of the inductive intellect; and (c) the outcome, i.e. the modern period.

He believed that humanity started in a phase of minority. Since it was yet to acquire inductive reasoning, psychic energy economized individual thought and choice by offering ready-made judgements, choices and ways of action through prophetic consciousness.[2] This changed with 'the birth of inductive intellect', signified by Islam.[3] Hence, Islam affirmed all previous revelations on the basis of a common essence, i.e. Unity; but it also declared that there would be no more prophets. This was a precaution against the 'formation and growth of non-rational modes of consciousness' (such as prophetic authority).[4]

Principle of Movement in the Structure of Islam'; and, added in the next edition: (g) 'Is Religion Possible?'

[1] In 1863, Syed Ahmad Khan (later Sir Syed) had pointed out that Christianity was not the enemy of Islam in modern times, and the real challenge was coming from modern philosophy (including modern science). Sir Syed proposed two possible strategies: either (a) to show that the precepts of religion were the same as those of modern science; or (b) to show that the domains of religion and science were different from each other. Iqbal addressed both approaches, but went a step beyond with the help of new evidence which had emerged since the times of Sir Syed.

[2] Lecture V in Iqbal (1930/1934), p.119

[3] Lecture V in Iqbal (1930/1934), p.120. In *Javid Nama*, inductive intellect is depicted as cumulative achievement of seven types of intelligences, symbolized by (a) Vedic philosophy (rational-intuitive intelligence); (b) Music (musical intelligence); (c) Poetry (linguistic intelligence); (d) Buddhism (body-soul intelligence); (e) Zoroastrianism (interpersonal intelligence); (f) Christianity (intrapersonal intelligence); and (g) Islam (spatial intelligence). See Iqbal (Persian; 1973), pp.619-644. For interpretation, Shafique (2007/2009), pp.137-152

[4] Lecture V in Iqbal (1930/1934), p.119

The process that started with it was still going on and at least three stages of further development could be discerned:

(a) *Motor-Sensory Stage.* The early Muslims found humanity to be in a 'motor-sensory' stage,[1] where human being was 'comparatively primitive and governed more or less by suggestion'.[2] Islam began to change this by fostering 'habits of concrete thought'[3] but they could not be cultivated completely at that time.

(b) *The Extension of Power.* There came a second phase (roughly corresponding to the period between the consolidation of the Mongol power after 1258 and the universal decline of monarchies in the eighteenth century). In this period, Europe discovered a new culture that, 'on its intellectual side' was 'a further development of some of the most important phases of the culture of Islam'. The outcome was 'infinite advance ... in the domain of human thought and experience' and the extension of the human power over nature.[4]

(c) *The Stage of Concrete Thought.* Thus acquiring 'a new faith and a fresh sense of superiority over the forces that constitute his environment',[5] human being entered the present phase in the eighteenth century.

This stage is signified by 'a concrete type of mind' and those 'habits of concrete thought' that Islam had 'fostered at least in the earlier stages of its cultural career'.[6] The outcome could be

---

[1] The Urdu phrase was خوگر پیکر محسوس , used in the poem 'Complaint'; see Iqbal (Urdu; 1973), p.164 [or Iqbal (Urdu; 1990), p.191]. Here, it has been translated as 'motor-sensory', a phrase popularized by the French psychologist Jean Piaget in the 1960s.
[2] Lecture V in Iqbal (1930/1934), p.120
[3] Preface in Iqbal (1930/1934), p.v
[4] Lecture I in Iqbal (1930/1934), p.7
[5] Lecture I in Iqbal (1930/1934), p.7
[6] Preface in Iqbal (1930/1934), p.v

the birth of a 'new human being', which Nature seemed to be creating in the deepest recesses of Life even at that time.[1]

Ijtihad

Iqbal addressed the specific requirements associated with the present stage of concrete thought by attempting to reconcile the categories of permanence and change, something that had not been achieved either by traditional Muslim thought or modern European political and social sciences (since the former had only emphasized permanence and the latter only change).[2]

He consolidated the ideas that he had been presenting since 1908, now embellishing them with an astounding range of references to contemporary Western writers, thinkers and scientists.[3] This provided the educated elite with an academic explanation of ideas that had already met the approval of the general body of the Indian Muslims, and which were shaping their collective life – new approaches to the Islamic conception of God, revelation, soul, destiny, and life after death; the practical implications of faith, and so on.

This reconciliation of the categories of permanence and change in religious thought led to a bigger idea: there should be

---

[1] Iqbal (Persian; 1973), p.182
[2] Lecture VI in Iqbal (1930/1934), pp.140-141
[3] Our of the numerous Western authors discussed in the book, many were either alive at that time or had lived in the twentieth century: Samuel Alexander, Henri Louis Bergson, Robert Briffault, Charlie Dunbar Broad, Herbert Wildon Carr, Carl Gustav Jung, Oswald Spengler, John Hopkins Denison, Hans Adolf Driesch, Arthur Stanley Eddington, Albert Einstein, L. Richard Farnell, Sigmund Freud, John Scott Haldane, Werner Karl Heisenberg, William Ernst Hocking, R. F. Alfred Hoernle, Max Horten, Snouck Hergronje, John Laird, Carl Georg Lange, Duncan Macdonald, Louis Massignon, John McTaggart Ellis McTaggart, Aghnides, Joseph Friedrich Naumann, Friedrich W. Nietzsche, T. Percy Nunn, Max Karl Ernst Ludwig Planck, Andrew Seth Pringle-Pattison, Louis Rougier, Arthur William Bertrand Russell, Halim Sabit, Hans Vaihinger, Alfred North Whitehead, Samuel Marinus Zwemer

Ijtihad, or reinterpretation of Muslim Law, and it should be carried out by the general will instead of individuals. Ijma, or consensus, was in his opinion 'the most important legal notion in Islam' but absolute monarchy had kept it suppressed throughout the history. This was likely to change now:

> ...the pressure of new world-forces and the political experience of European nations are impressing on the mind of modern Islam the value and possibilities of the idea of Ijma. The growth of republican spirit and the gradual formation of legislative assemblies in Muslim lands constitute a great step in advance. The transfer of the power of Ijtihad from individual representatives of schools to a Muslim legislative assembly that, in view of the growth of opposing sects, is the only possible form Ijma can take in modern times, will secure contributions to legal discussion from laymen who happen to possess a keen insight into affairs. In this way alone can we stir into activity the dormant spirit of life in our legal system, and give it an evolutionary outlook.[1]

Thus the concepts of mutual consultation and self-determination became linked with the grand vision of an elected assembly reinterpreting the Muslim Law. The Ulema (religious scholars) could guide such an assembly 'only as a temporary measure in Sunni countries'.[2] The permanent remedy was 'to reform the present system of legal education in Muhammadan countries, to extend its sphere, and to combine it with an intelligent study of modern jurisprudence.'[3]

---

[1] Iqbal (1934/1939), p.165
[2] The Iranian constitution of 1906 had provided a supervisory role for an ecclesiastical committee, which Iqbal regarded as 'probably necessary in view of the Persian constitutional theory' but did not recommend it for Sunni countries where that theory did not apply. See Iqbal (1934/1939), pp.166-167
[3] Iqbal (1934/1939), p.167

Sources of inspiration

The lectures drew upon three potent authorities:

a. the general will of the Muslim community, which had partially expressed itself in 'spiritually moving towards the West' for regaining its hold on matter;[1]

b. modern science and philosophy, especially 'the more recent developments';

c. the philosophical traditions of Islam and its theological thought – which needed revision and reconstruction.[2]

He deliberately kept out the fourth prominent trend of those days – atheistic socialism or Bolshevism – although it had 'all the fervour of a new religion' and even had 'a broader outlook'.[3] In spite of writing later that 'Bolshevism plus God is almost identical with Islam',[4] he had reasons to think that it should not be a source of inspiration for Muslim thought or literature.[5]

---

[1] Lecture I in Iqbal (1930/1934), p.7; and Iqbal (1967/1981), p.82
[2] Lecture I in Iqbal (1930/1934), p.7
[3] Lecture VII in Iqbal (1930/1934), p.178
[4] Iqbal (1977/1995), p.250
[5] Five reasons can be gathered from his writings: (a) 'Scientific materialism' on which Bolshevism was originally based, appeared to be 'rapidly disappearing' even in the domain of modern science [Lecture II, Iqbal (1930/1934), p.32]; (b) Islam has its own economic ideal: unlike capitalism, it discourages the concentration of capital; but unlike atheistic socialism, it aims at channelling the capital rather than eliminating its private ownership altogether [Open letter published in Urdu in 1923]; (c) The channelling of the economic activity in Islam was to be achieved through the elimination of fear, on the premise that self-respect, fearlessness and freedom would invariably lead human being to 'respect the personalities of others and become perfectly virtuous' [Iqbal (1977/1995), p.103]; (d) 'having received its philosophical basis from the Hegelians of the left wing', Bolshevism failed to address the soul (and personality), and negated it along with the existence of God; therefore, it lacked strength and purpose [Lecture VII in Iqbal (1930/1934), p.178], aiming only at the 'equality of stomachs' (whereas Islam aimed at the equality of souls). [Iqbal (Persian; 1973), p.652]; (e) 'both nationalism and atheistic socialism, at least in the present state of human adjustments, must draw upon the psychological forces of hate, suspicion, and resentment which tend to impoverish the soul of

Reception

The first round of the lectures was presided over by a non-Muslim, Dr. P. Subharoyan. While admitting his surprise at his nomination 'to preside over a meeting like this', he expressed pleasure as 'an Indian and a believer in the existence of a common God who has created the entire world'.[1] A student body at Aligarh declared the book to be 'the greatest, the noblest and the finest gospel that our age has to give – the radiation of Islam as understood and interpreted by one of the most comprehensive and inspired intellects of the modern world'.[2]

Allahabad Address (1930)

The same process of 'careful study of Islam' that had produced the lectures of the *Reconstruction,* was supposed to be the source of insight that he offered as the president of the All-India Muslim League – on the first day of the annual session of the party in Allahabad on December 29-30, 1930.[3] Originally in English, the presidential address is best remembered as the occasion where the poet-philosopher proposed and predicted the birth of 'a consolidated North-West Indian Muslim state'.[4]

---

man and close up his hidden sources of spiritual energy'. [Lecture VII in Iqbal (1930/1934), p.178]

[1] Iqbal (1967/1981), p.50

[2] Iqbal (1967/1981), p.101

[3] For historical information, records and original text in English, see Nadeem Shafique Malik (2013). For an annotated text in English, see Shafique (2006/2007), pp.135-148.

[4] Shafique (2006/2007), p.138

The road to Allahabad

The election of 1926 had given landslide victory to the Hindu Mahasabha, which was avowedly opposed to the existence of the Indian Muslims as a distinct community. One of its major demands was the repudiation of separate electorates. The Muslims were now forced to look for alternatives to separate electorates. The process started with a meeting of Muslim leaders in Delhi in March 1927.[1]

The Congress could not afford to ignore the Mahasabha either. In the Nehru Report, flaunted by the Congress in 1928 as the proposed constitution for India, separate electorates were repudiated on the grounds that the existence of the Indian Muslims as a distinct community was incompatible with the unity of India. This was contrary to the position the Congress had adopted in the Lucknow Pact twelve years ago. It was also a final refutation of the grand vision that had been unfolding through the more pragmatic nationalists such as C. R. Das (regrettably dead by then) and Muhammad Ali Jauhar (who now bid farewell to Congress, along with a very large number of other Muslim leaders).

In this atmosphere of amnesia and confusion, Iqbal teased out the self-contradictions in the positions of the major political contestants and spelled out the logical conclusion on which all diverse opinions seemed to be converging, some inadvertently.[2]

---

[1] Its proposals were modified into Fourteen Points by Jinnah two years later, and were backed by Iqbal.

[2] Iqbal's proposition was different from that of Lala Lajpat Rai and some others which came afterwards: (a) Iqbal did not desire the partitions of Punjab and Bengal; (b) his proposal did not imply transfer of population; (c) he aimed at a composite nation of several religions adhering to a common ethical ideal; (d) while Rai had focused only on religion, Iqbal aimed 'to secure comparatively homogeneous communities possessing linguistic, racial, cultural and religious unity.'

Muslim state

The logical conclusion, as it appeared to him, was worded by him as a proposition as well as a prediction:

> *I would like to see the Punjab, North-West Frontier Province, Sind and Baluchistan amalgamated into a single state.[1] Self-Government within the British Empire, or without the British Empire, the formation of a consolidated North-West Indian Muslim state appears to me to be the final destiny of the Muslims at least of the North-West India.[2]*

Morally, the proposition could be justified on the basis of international law as understood at that time.[3] The largest Muslim community of the world lived in India, and was not getting a chance to represent itself even in those areas where it was in majority. The Northwest Frontier Province (92% Muslim population) and Baluchistan (88% Muslim population) had not been granted constitutional reforms on the same footing as the rest of British India. Sindh (71% Muslim population) was not even a province, and was an appendage of the Bombay Presidency. The boundaries of Punjab had been drawn in such a manner that Muslims were left with a small majority (57%), and that too had been rendered ineffective due to political intrigues.[4]

With the rearrangement suggested by Iqbal, the Indian Muslims may not have required any further persuasion for giving up separate electorates. They were already a majority in Bengal, and the consolidation of the four provinces on the other

---

[1] This is the most oft-quoted passage on the basis of which this address is regarded as the foundation stone of Pakistan.
[2] Shafique (2006/2007), p.138-139
[3] Such as the Fourteen Points of the American President Johnson, the widely respected basis for international relations at that time.
[4] Hafeez Malik (2009), p.6

side of the Indian subcontinent into a Muslim majority state would mean two powerful units – one on either side – where Muslims would be enjoying the democratic privileges of a majority. 'For India it means security and peace resulting from the internal balance of power.' This is how Iqbal saw it.[1]

Javid Nama (1932)

Around the time when he was working on the address to be delivered in Allahabad, he was also composing what would become the fifth book of his poetry and his greatest masterpiece, *Javid Nama*. It was an epic in Persian and was self-published from Lahore in February 1932.[2] It could be seen as providing the bigger picture of which the ideal state proposed and predicted by him in the presidential address was a part.

The book may have originated as 'The Future Life of Islam', mentioned in the private correspondence of the poet in 1917.[3] The format was suggested by the incident of Meraj – the accession of the Prophet to heavens, which Iqbal termed as 'unitary experience'.[4] What was 'culturally speaking, more important' to him was 'the intense appeal that the story has always made to the average Muslim, and the manner in which Muslim thought and imagination have worked on it'.[5] A large number of mystics and writers had written about their own

---

[1] Shafique (2006/2007), p.139
[2] Now included in Iqbal (Persian; 1973), pp.589-796. For publication history, see Shafique (2006/2007), pp.160-163 and Hashmi (Urdu; 1982/2010), pp.170-171.
[3] This is my inference, based on a study of Iqbal's manuscripts. Details are going to be presented in the forthcoming publication in Urdu, *Iqbal: Daur-i-Urooj*.
[4] Lecture V in Iqbal (1930/1934), p.118
[5] Razzaqi (1979/2003), p.122

unitary experiences. It had also been suggested by the Spanish scholar Miguel Ausin in *Divine Comedy and Islam* (1919) that the story of Meraj, through Ibn-ul-Arabi, was a major influence on the medieval Italian poet Dante for his *Divine Comedy* (although Dante treated the Prophet and his cousin Ali with prejudice in his book).

In Iqbal's epic, diverse themes such as the quest for immortality, a meeting with God and the destiny of nations came together in a carefully woven plot. It was essentially an allegory about the life of the author and the future of the world in which he was living. No wonder that the book was specifically addressed to the youth, symbolically addressed by the name of the poet's younger son, Javid, which literally meant 'the eternal' (relationship with the elder son Aftab had strained beyond repair by this time).

The plot

Three pre-requisites for immortality are given by the character of Rumi in the story as (a) seeing oneself through one's own vision; (b) seeing oneself through the light of the vision of another; and (c) seeing oneself through the eyes of God.[1]

The process takes the poet through seven stages under the guidance of his mentor, Rumi, who has given him the nickname 'the Living Stream' (Zindah Rud).[2] At each stage, the traveller keeps finding a new piece of information about how to create a perfect world, or what impediments could get in its way (and these are basically the same as what the poet-philosopher had been giving to his nation through his other writings). The desired world is represented by 'Marghdeen', an imaginary city on Mars.

---

[1] Iqbal (Persian; 1973), p.607
[2] Iqbal (Persian; 1973), p.649

At the end of the journey, God Himself reveals the secret of immortality: 'Be vital, be creative. Like Me, embrace all horizons.'[1] Hence the achievement of immortality becomes conditional on one's contribution to the creation of Marghdeen – that perfect world, the clues of which were being given throughout the story.[2]

Marghdeen

The name was of Iqbal's coinage, but could be traced to the words *margh* and *deen,* roughly connoting 'the Pasture of Religion'[1]. The legend, as presented in the fourth chapter, had three major aspects:

   a. Barkhia, a Martian, refused the temptation offered by Farzmurz, which was a world unknown to God and therefore free of His law.
   b. God rewarded the descendants of Barkhia with an inside-out existence: they transcended the dichotomy of body and spirit, lived soulfully and could happily foretell their deaths a few days in advance.
   c. The Marghdeen of Barkhia was the name of their city, which was free from crime, injustice or poverty (as described in more detail in the prologue of the present volume).

It should not be difficult to see that all three elements are allegorical references to issues that were confronting Iqbal and his community at that time, and had been discussed even in his famous presidential address.

---

[1] Iqbal (Persian; 1973), p.779.
[2] This moral of the story is not unlike how Sir Syed had linked 'the good deed that lasts forever' and 'the soul of all human beings' with serving 'the entire humankind, especially one's own community' See Panipati, ed. (1990), p.261

Farzmurz obviously symbolized European political thinking, with its roots in the philosophy of Machiavelli instead of Christ's vision of human brotherhood, resulting in states 'dominated by interests, not human but national.' Just as Farzmurz approached Barkhia with an offer, 'the ideas set free by European political thinking' were also 'rapidly changing the outlook of the present generation of Muslims both in India and outside India.'[2]

The offer made by Farzmurz in the story was a world about which he claimed to be unknown to God, and therefore free from the fetters of the Divine Law. In the presidential address, Iqbal had mentioned the same offer being made by European political thinking: 'Is religion a private affair? Would you like to see Islam, as a moral and political ideal, meeting the same fate in the world of Islam as Christianity has already met in Europe? Is it possible to retain Islam as an ethical ideal and to reject it as a polity in favour of national polities in which religious attitude is not permitted to play any part?'[3]

In the story, Barkhia rejects the offer of Farzmurz. In his presidential address, Iqbal had asked the Indian Muslims to do the same: '...the construction of a polity on national lines, if it means a displacement of the Islamic principle of solidarity, is simply unthinkable to a Muslim. This is a matter which at the present moment directly concerns the Muslims of India.' To make the choice that Barkhia made in the story, the community of Iqbal had to reject the European concept of state.

However, Iqbal never spelled out any details of the political system that his community should adopt instead. The system had

---

[1] This connotation was suggested to me by M. Suheyl Umar in a conversation.
[2] Shafique (2006/2007), p.136
[3] He insisted that this was not a purely theoretical problem, but 'a proper solution of it alone depends your future as a distinct cultural unit in India ... Never in our history Islam has had to stand a greater trial than the one which confronts it today.'

to evolve gradually through the collective will. In the presidential address, he had only informed his readers that 'things in India are not what they appear to be. The meaning of this, however, will dawn upon you only when you have achieved a real collective ego to look at them.'[1]

In other words, the community would become capable of seeing the alternative system only after it has been rewarded by God in the same manner as the progeny of Barkhia. In the story, they were given a soulful mode of life, which enabled them to foresee their own deaths without regret. This was obviously an allegorical reference to Iqbal's long-held belief that 'the very number of days' which an individual lives was 'determined by the needs of the community.'[2] To foresee one's own death without regret was, then, a symbolic manner of depicting an individual's awareness about his or her role in the collective life, and his or her contentment about having fulfilled that role.[3] It is what Iqbal mentioned elsewhere as 'a living experience of the kind of biological unity' implied in the verse of the Quran: 'Your creation and resurrection are like the creation and resurrection of a single soul.'[1]

The remarkable city of Marghdeen, with its material abundance and spiritual bliss, was actually the inevitable outcome of such consciousness. In the story, this is explained by

---

[1] Shafique (2006/2007), p.148
[2] Iqbal (1977/1995), p.119
[3] Iqbal may have felt the need for this detail in order to differentiate his idea of soulful living from that type of mysticism which was 'supposed to be a life-denying, fact-avoiding attitude of mind directly opposed to the radically empirical outlook of our times.'[3] Far from remedying any ills, such an attitude was actually the mother of the evils which Barkhia was supposed to fight: 'If you begin with the conception of religion as complete other-worldliness, then what has happened to Christianity in Europe is perfectly natural. The universal ethics of Jesus is displaced by national systems of ethics and polity.' See Shafique (2006/2007), p.136

a Martian astronomer who says to the travellers from the earth that the material objects come from the same source as the power of thought and the potency of prayer. Therefore, whatever is earned by one through one's efforts is a trust given by the Almighty. 'Why is there poverty and want on earth?' The Martian asks rhetorically, and goes on to answer, 'Because you claim as yours what belongs to God. Therefore, you cannot tell goal from path, otherwise the value of everything is measured by the regard given to it by *you*. A gem is a gem as long as you think it is valuable, otherwise it is just a stone. The world will shape itself according to your perception of it. The heavens and the earth too will adjust.'

Lahore Address (1932)

These were the wider implications of the programme that Iqbal had placed before his community in his presidential address of 1930. He reiterated that programme soon after the publication of *Javid Nama,* when he presided over the annual session of the All-India Muslim Conference in Lahore in March 1932.[2] The conference had emerged as a common platform for four Muslim political parties, and had been formed by Iqbal's old class fellow and prominent politician Sir Fazli Husain with support from His Highness Aga Khan III.

In his presidential address to the conference, which is also called the *Lahore Address,* Iqbal declared that 'the issues have fortunately become so clear that the whole thing now depends not so much on the guidance of one particular individual as on

---

[1] Iqbal (1930/1934), p.v . The quotation from Quran is Chapter 31 'Luqman', Verse 28.
[2] Included in Iqbal (1977/1995), pp.30-49

the force of all the individual wills focused on a single purpose'.[1] The purpose, in his words, was:

> ... no communal settlement, provisional or permanent, can satisfy the Muslim community, which does not recognize, as its basic principle, the right of the community to enjoy majority rights in provinces where it happens to be in actual majority.[2]

A political cultural programme

Placing all the blame of chaos in Muslim politics on the leaders, and absolving the masses unconditionally, he proposed a 'partly political, partly cultural' program based on five points. Parts of this programme were eventually put into practice by Jinnah in the next decade with considerable success:

1   The Indian Muslims should have only one political organization with accommodations for various political schools of thought.
2   This organization should gather a national fund of at least five million rupees.
3   It should have youth leagues and well-equipped volunteer corps for cultural and economic awareness among the peasants with a futuristic approach.

---

[1] Iqbal (1977/1995), p.31
[2] Iqbal (1977/1995), p.36. This was echoed in the famous Lahore Resolution adopted by the All-India Muslim League eight years later: '... no constitutional plan would be workable in this country or acceptable to Muslims unless ... geographically contiguous units are demarcated into regions which should be so constituted ... that the areas in which the Muslims are numerically in a majority ... should be grouped to constitute "Independent States" in which the constituent units shall be autonomous and sovereign.' See text text in Ahmad (2006), pp.290-291

4   It should set up segregated cultural institutes for men and women throughout the country 'to mobilize the spiritual energy of the younger generation' while keeping close touch with the old and new education institutions.

5   There should be an assembly of ulema and modern Muslim lawyers for scrutinizing all bills on Muslim personal law, bringing out the undiscovered possibilities of the Islamic law in solving the economic problems of the world.[1]

Foreign travels

Iqbal took three trips abroad during the early 1930s. The first two were in connection with the Second and Third Round Table Conferences held in London, respectively in 1931 and 1932. The third trip was to the neighbouring state of Afghanistan on a special invitation by King Nadir Shah for advising on the education policy of that state.

Gandhi

The Third Round Table Conference brought Iqbal into a conflict with Mohandas Karamchand Gandhi, who was the sole representative of the Congress on that occasion. Unfortunately, these two giants, who were both striving for discovering peaceful means for achieving political freedom, failed to see eye to eye. Ultimately, their differences could be traced back to the fact that Gandhi accepted race as the basis of nationality while Iqbal perceived a nation to be based on 'the psychological fact

---

[1] Iqbal (1977/1995), pp.45-49

of like-mindedness'.[1] Just like Rousseau, he also believed the state to be a contractual organism.[2] For the same reason, Iqbal could not concede to Gandhi's insistence that Muslim leaders should not support the scheduled castes in their demand for separate electorates.

In spite of their political differences, Iqbal and Gandhi continued to extend courtesy to each other.[3]

Writing inspired by foreign travels

Iqbal received much attention as a poet-philosopher during his travels, and met celebrities including the exiled King Amanullah of Afghanistan, the former Iranian Prime Minister Tabatabatai and the Italian dictator Benito Mussolini. His desire to travel through Germany could not materialize, apparently due to suspected surveillance by British intelligence.

His communication with Emma Wegenast, if it had been disrupted, resumed on these occasions and included such painful letters about regrettable changes in itineraries:

> It was extremely kind of you to write and I was looking forward to meeting you at Heidelberg. I am, however, extremely sorry to tell you that in view of sudden changes necessitated in my programme it is not now possible to pass through Germany .... It would have given me immense pleasure to meet you once more in life and to revive old associations, but, as ill luck would have it, this has become impossible...

---

[1] Iqbal (1977/1995), p.141

[2] Iqbal (1977/1995), p.147; Shafique (2006/2007), p.139

[3] While in London during the Third Round Table Conference, Gandhi attended a reception given in honour of Iqbal as a poet-philosopher. On other occasions, he mentioned affectionately that the patriotic poems of Iqbal had been a source of solace and moral strength for him in his difficult march towards freedom.

He not written any poetry in Urdu after 1923, but practically every stopover in these journeys inspired some short or long poem in Urdu. These poems, which went into the sixth and seventh books of his poetry (*Gabriel's Wing* and *The Blow of Moses*), are replete with passionate references to France, England, Italy, Palestine, Egypt, Spain and Afghanistan.

In addition, he also wrote some papers and articles for the European audience and a versified travelogue of Afghanistan in Persian.[1] Some of these memorabilia of the travels surpassed his previous work in fame and popularity. The poem 'The Mosque of Cordoba', written as a result of his visit to Spain, is generally considered to be the greatest poem ever written in Urdu.

Retirement

On January 10, 1934, Iqbal caught cold while offering the congregational prayer of Eid in the Badshahi Mosque, Lahore. The first symptom was a partial loss of voice, rendering him unable to pursue his legal career or even to address mass meetings with his soul-stirring poetry or addresses. Initially, it was suspected to be influenza but turned out to be a prolonged illness that gradually rendered him bed-ridden. Later, he also developed cataract, which prevented him from reading and writing. He died of cardiac asthma in April 1938. In spite of these physical handicaps, the last four years of his life were far from unproductive.

---

[1] Most of the papers and writings addressed to European audience are to be found in Iqbal (1967/1981), Iqbal (1977/1995) and Iqbal (1979/2003). Lecture delivered before the Aristotelian Society, London, was included as Lecture VII in Iqbal (1930/1934). The versified Persian travelogue was the masnavi 'Traveler' (Musafir), Iqbal (Persian; 1973), pp.849-882

His third wife, Sirdar Begum, had shared his personal trait of frugality. Her savings and jewellery turned out to be sufficient for purchasing a land and constructing a house on it, which was completed in 1935. It was called Javid Manzil, after their son, Javid.[1] Iqbal made sure that the house should be in the name of Sirdar. Unfortunately, she had fallen very ill sometime before the completion of the house, where she was brought on a stretcher on May 20, 1935.[2] On Iqbal's advice, she transferred the property to her ten year old son before breathing her last three days after moving into the new house. Iqbal became a tenant of his young son and regularly deposited the amount of the monthly rent in the child's bank account.[3]

Sirdar's death came as a great blow. Iqbal never got over it completely. He believed that the spirit of the departed wife was in touch with him.[4] Also, he stopped dyeing his hair. He entertained no thoughts of remarrying, and instead hired a German governess, Mrs. Doris Ahmad, to look after the two children, Javid and Munira.

Moral and economic support came from Bhopal. Sir Ross Masud, grandson of the great Sir Syed, had recently become the Education Minister of the princely state. The ruler, Nawab Hamidullah Khan, was well-known for his devotion to the cause of Muslim Renaissance and excelled in personal courtesy. On the suggestion of Sir Ross, he issued a monthly stipend of five hundred rupees for Iqbal, in addition to arrangements for electrotherapy in the state's hospital. This was the only instance when Iqbal accepted stipend from a prince. He politely stopped Sir Ross from seeking additional support from three other potential patrons.

---

[1] Dr. Hafeez Malik (2009), p.310
[2] Dr. Hafeez Malik (2009), p.310
[3] Dr. Hafeez Malik (2009), p.310
[4] See Niazi (1971)

While his legal practice was thus discontinued, his literary pursuit and political activism continued to flourish. When cataract prevented him from reading and writing, he turned to assistance from secretaries – young volunteers who were only too happy to be helpful. Lying down in his bedroom in Javid Manzil, he received important visitors including Muhammad Ali Jinnah, Lord Lothian, Tej Bahadur Sapru, and Jawaharlal Nehru. He saw his works getting published – including an Oxford University Press edition of the *Reconstruction,* four new books of poetry and a series of articles and press statements. He accepted the personal request of Jinnah to join the Central Parliamentary Board of the All-India Muslim League in 1936. Later, he also became the president of its provincial branch in Punjab and played 'a very conspicuous part, though at the time not revealed to public', in organizing the Muslim community 'as one party with an advanced and progressive programme'.[1]

The Reconstruction of Religious Thought in Islam (1934)

A revised second edition of the lectures came out from Oxford University Press in May 1934 as *The Reconstruction of Religious Thought in Islam* (dropping the 'Six Lectures on' from the title).[2] Revisions in the text were minor, except the addition of a completely new lecture that had been delivered at London at the request of the Aristotelian Society in 1932.

Gabriel's Wing (1935)

The sixth book of his poetry, *Gabriel's Wing* (Baal-i-Jibreel) was in Urdu and was self-published in January 1935 from

---

[1] Jinnah's foreword to the anthology of letters written to him by Iqbal; Iqbal (1943/2001), pp.7-8
[2] Hashmi (Urdu; 1982/2010), pp.320-321

Lahore.[1] It soon became one of the most highly acclaimed poetical works in Urdu, unsurpassed as a combination of philosophical themes, powerful expression and moving melody.

The book carried a visible affinity with the two works that had preceded it. Its greatest poem, 'The Mosque of Cordoba', illustrated the views about art and architecture propounded in *Persian Psalms,* and is often treated as if it were architecture of words. The landscape of *Javid Nama* continued to provide cosmology for the new book, so that *Gabriel's Wing* could easily be taken as an account of the return journey from 'the Divine Presence' where *Javid Nama* had ended.[2]

The war of literature

In spite of the immense popularity of Iqbal, the 'Islamic Movement' of Indian literature to which he belonged was like a solitary ray of hope due to lack of funds at the disposal of its parent community. A comprehensive scheme for setting up an Iqbal Academy was published by Raghib Muradabadi, a young intellectual from Calcutta, in 1932. Iqbal himself had proposed setting up cultural institutes in his *Lahore Address* of the same year. None of these suggestions could be materialized.

By the mid-1930s, other forces entered the competition with more glamour at their disposal. The first meeting of the All-India Progressive Writers' Association was held in Lucknow on April 10, 1936, inside the venue of the annual session of the Indian National Congress, and with the blessings of Jawaharlal Nehru. The aims of the movement included 'combating literary

---

[1] Now included in Iqbal (Urdu; 1973), pp.293-462 [or Iqbal (Urdu; 1990), p.325-500]. For publication history, see Shafique (2006/2007), p.184 and Hashmi (Urdu; 1982/2010), pp.59-62.

[2] This is my inference.

trends reflecting communalism'.[1] It was further stated in the presidential address that 'Buddha, Christ, Muhammad, all the prophets, tried without success to lay the foundation of their equality on moral precepts without any success ... We shall fail again if we attempt to attain our goal with the help of religion'.[2]

An 'Islamic Movement' of literature had little chance to be carried forward by the adherents of this new trend, which lured away a galaxy of the most creative and brilliant minds among the youth of Muslim India.[3] Nor could the Islamic Movement of Literature find home in the camp of those among the intellectual elite who were opposed to the left-leaning Progressive Movement. Halqa-i-Arbab-i-Zauq, also set up in 1936, was opposed to Marxist ideas about literature but sought its inspiration from contemporary Europe (that according to Iqbal had long lost the capability of bringing forth any 'healthy literary ideal'[4]). Muhammad Hasan Askari, a champion of Muslim culture among the intellectual elite, was soon going to condemn Sir Syed and Hali, and disown their legacy on the grounds that it was inspired by European ideas.

Iqbal criticised the new intelligentsia in *The Blow of Moses*, his 'declaration of war against the present age' (discussed later in this chapter). However, his efforts in the final years of his life were focussed more on securing for the Muslim masses the most important thing that he feared was being taken away from them: their right to self-determination.

---

[1] Dr. Hafeez Malik (1967), pp.650-651
[2] Dr. Hafeez Malik (1967), p.650
[3] Dr. Hafeez Malik (1967), p.652
[4] Preface to *The Message of the East* in Iqbal (Persian; 1973), p.182

Kashmir

The princely state of Jammu and Kashmir had a predominantly Muslim population (around 70% altogether but more than 90% in the valley of Kashmir). It was ruled by a Hindu dynasty, to which the British had sold the valley and its people for 7.5 million rupees in 1846. The dynasty was unpopular and the people revolted in the early 1930s. An All-India Kashmir Committee was formed in British India and, as its president, Iqbal appealed to the people of Kashmir to unite their ranks: 'The supreme need of the moment is a single party representing all Muslims in the State. If perfect unanimity of political opinion is not secured in Kashmir, all efforts of leaders to advance the interests of the people of the State will prove ineffective'.[1]

Ahmadis (also called Qadianis), who followed a religious movement founded by Mirza Ghulam Ahmad Qadiani in Punjab in the 1870s, were active in the Kashmir Committee but adopted a policy that Iqbal interpreted to mean that they recognized 'no loyalty except to the head of their particular religious sect'.[2] In the absence of a definite clarification from the Ahmadi headquarters, Iqbal expelled them from the Committee, in consistence with the long-held principle that the general opinion of the community must be the final arbiter for deciding the course of collective action. A little later, when a popular demand arose among the Muslims that the Ahmadis should be declared non-Muslims, and the Governor of Punjab reprimanded the Muslims for being intolerant, Iqbal defended the Muslim masses in public statements against the Governor and the enlightened elite.[3]

---

[1] Iqbal (1977/1995), p.277

[2] Iqbal (1977/1995), p. 279

[3] The average Muslims, according to Iqbal, even if inspired by sheer instinct of collective self-preservation, were fighting for universal emancipation in the sense that the idea of the Finality of Prophethood was 'perhaps the most original idea in the cultural history of mankind'.. See Iqbal (1977/1995), p. 198

Jawaharlal Nehru and his father had been praised in *Javid Nama,* and Nehru retained a cordial relationship with Iqbal till the end, but three articles by Nehru in the *Modern Review,* Calcutta, in November and December 1935, were filled with biting sarcasm. Apparently with an aim of alienating Sir Aga Khan III from the masses, he also bracketed the Ismaili sect of Aga Khan with Ahmadism. Rhetorically, but powerfully, he contended that the 'solidarity of Islam' did not exist:

> ... I presume that Turkey under the Ataturk Kemal has certainly ceased to be an Islamic country in any sense of the word. Egypt has been powerfully influenced by religious reformers who have tried to put on new garments on the ancient truths, and, I imagine, that Sir Mohamad [Iqbal] does not approve of this modernist tendency. The Arabs of Syria and Palestine more or less follow Egyptian thought-currents and are partly influenced by Turkey's example. Iran is definitely looking for its cultural inspiration to pre-Islamic Magian days. In all these countries, indeed in every country of western and middle Asia, nationalist ideas are rapidly growing, usually at the expense of the pure and orthodox religious outlook. Islam, as Sir Mohamad tells us, repudiates the race idea (and of course the geographical idea) and founds itself on the religious idea alone. But in the Islamic countries of western Asia we find today the race and geographical ideas all-powerful. The Turk takes pride in the Turanian race; the Iranian in his own ancient racial traditions; the Egyptian and Syrian (as well as the people of Palestine, Trans-Jordan and Iraq) dream of Arab unity in which the Muslim and Christian Arabs will share.
>
> All this clearly shows that these nations have fallen away from the ideal of Islamic solidarity which Sir Mohamad lays down. Where then does this

solidarity exist at present? Not in Central Asia, for in the Soviet parts the breakaway from orthodoxy is far greater; in the Chinese parts the predominant currents are probably nationalist (Turanian) and Soviet. Afghanistan and Arabia proper remain in Asia, and then there are a number of Islamic countries in North Africa, apart from Egypt. How far this orthodox outlook of religious solidarity is prevalent there I do not know, but reports indicate that nationalistic ideas have penetrated even there. And nationalism and the solidarity of Islam do not fit in side by side. Each weakens the other ... The Aga Khan, we are told, is the leader of Indian Muslims. Does he stand for this solidarity of Islam as defined by Sir Mohamad Iqbal?[1]

'Islam and Ahmadism' (1936)

Iqbal responded with 'Islam and Ahmadism', a scholarly paper published in three instalments in the *Islam,* Lahore, in January 1936 (and widely circulated as a pamphlet in Urdu as well).[2]

Boldly, he stated that 'not one' out of the hundreds of writers who had written about modern Islam understood 'the nature of the effect or of the cause that has brought about that effect'.[3] Contrary to their views, Iqbal insisted that the recent developments in the world of Islam (such as those mentioned by Nehru) were 'wholly determined by the forces within' even if 'pressure of modern ideas may be admitted'. Leaders who had brought about these changes were actually playing on the grounds prepared by the reformers of the previous century.

---

[1] 'Solidarity of Islam – comment on Iqbal's Article'. Source: *Cultural and Religious Heritage of India: Islam.* edited by Suresh K. Sharma, Usha Sharma, pp.285-287
[2] Included in Iqbal (1977/1995), p.214-240
[3] Iqbal (1977/1995), p.229

'Such men are liable to make mistakes;' he wrote, 'but the history of nations shows that even their mistakes have sometimes borne good fruit. In them it is not logic but life that struggles restless to solve its own problems'.[1]

The Blow of Moses (1936)

The same ideas turned into Urdu poems comprising the seventh book of Iqbal's poetry, The Blow of Moses (Zarb-i-Kaleem), subtitled 'a declaration of war against the present age'. It was self-published from Lahore in July 1936.[2] It was dedicated to Nawab Hamidullah of Bhopal in gratitude for financial support.

In the light of Iqbal's lifelong stance that the spirit of modern times was wholly in keeping with the spirit of Islam,[3] the war declared in the subtitle is not against the spirit of modern times but against those poets, philosophers, saints and statesmen who receive inspiration from decadence itself, and unconsciously clothe despair in the glittering garment of hope.[4]

Thus, in the strongest possible words, he condemns the Grand Mosque of Paris (inaugurated in 1926 on behalf of the French colonial empire).[5] He also discourages the preaching of Islam in Europe, and proposes that the exploitation of the poorer nations would not end by the conversion of the white races since the Western political system was based on race itself rather than religion: 'The Brahmin does not increase in stature in the eyes of

---

[1] Iqbal (1977/1995), p. 232

[2] Now included in Iqbal (Urdu; 1973), pp.463-641 [or Iqbal (Urdu; 1990), pp.501-692]. For publication history, see Shafique (2006/2007), p.185 and Hashmi (Urdu; 1982/2010), p.65.

[3] Reiterated in his rejoinders to Nehru, when the book was about to go into print. See Iqbal (1977/1995), p.237

[4] Iqbal (Urdu; 1973), pp.602-603 [or Iqbal (Urdu; 1990), p.652]; see also Iqbal (1977/1995), pp.227-228

[5] Iqbal (Urdu; 1990), p.615

the Englishman by embracing the religion of the Christ.'[1] On the whole, the book reflects an anxiety that European colonialism may leave behind the nationalist India and the proposed state of Israel as two agents through whom it could continue to undermine the solidarity of the Muslim world.[2] The remedies, as also suggested in other statements around this time, were: (a) reunion of the Turks and the Arabs;[3] and (b) making Tehran the diplomatic headquarter of a united East.[4]

In the age of suicide attacks in the first quarter of the 21st Century, Iqbal's advice to the Palestinian Muslims seems to be acquiring an eerie relevance, where he asks them to seek political freedom through self-development and through 'the sheer joy of being alive'.[5] The twenty monologues of Mihrab Gul Afghan (a fictitious character from what is now the tribal area of Pakistan) also read like clippings from recent newspapers, but they also depict the gradual evolution of a synthetic perspective not very different from what is now emerging in the political discourse of the region.[6]

---

[1] Iqbal (Urdu; 1973), p.524 [or Iqbal (Urdu; 1990), pp.575-576]. These words, printed in Urdu in 1936, were corroborated in the next decade when T.S. Eliot wrote: 'If Asia were converted to Christianity tomorrow, it would not thereby become a part of Europe ... To our Christian heritage we owe many things besides religious faith.' See 'The Unity of European Culture' in *Christianity and Culture* by T. S. Eliot

[2] Iqbal (Urdu; 1973), pp.618-619 [or Iqbal (Urdu; 1990), p.668-669]. Also, on December 6, 1933, he had said publicly, 'either the Indian majority community will have to accept for itself the permanent position of an agent of British imperialism in the East or the country will have to be redistributed on a basis of religious, historical and cultural affinities...'; see Iqbal (1977/1995), p.290.

[3] Iqbal (1977/1995), p.295

[4] Iqbal (Urdu; 1973), p.609 [or Iqbal (Urdu; 1990), p.659]

[5] Iqbal (Urdu; 1973), p.622 [or Iqbal (Urdu; 1990), p.671]

[6] Iqbal (Urdu; 1973), pp.163-179 [or Iqbal (Urdu; 1990), pp.673-691]

Muhammad Ali Jinnah

Iqbal perceived Ataturk to be acting on the grounds prepared by Syed Jamal-ud-Din Afghani. It requires a shorter leap of imagination to associate Muhammad Ali Jinnah with Sir Syed Ahmad Khan, and hence see him as representing the same current of thought of which Iqbal had become the greatest icon by the time Jinnah made his comeback on the political scene of British India in the late 1933.

Jinnah was born in Karachi in 1876 and received early education in a school that was modelled after the Aligarh college of Sir Syed. After a stint in England in the 1890s, he returned as a barrister-at-law from the Lincoln's Inn (from where Iqbal was also called to bar later). Although a member of the Indian National Congress, his election to the Viceroy's legislative council had been as a Muslim representative and he proved his loyalty to his constituency by successfully pleading for the revival of an antiquated Muslim law in 1911 (having received guidance from Maulana Shibili Numani in preparing the brief). He became widely known as 'the Ambassador of Hindu-Muslim Unity' after engineering the Lucknow Pact in 1916. However, Iqbal remained sceptical of these achievements of Jinnah. Later on, he sided with Mian Sir Muhammad Shafi in the opposite camp during the temporary split in the Muslim League from 1927 to 1930.[1] He was present at the meeting in Delhi where Jinnah was supposed to present his fourteen points (but which had to be presented afterwards, due to disruption in the meeting). This brought him closer to the viewpoint of Iqbal, whom he nominated for presiding over the next annual session of the League, held at Allahabad in 1930, where Iqbal proposed and predicted the birth of a Muslim state.

---

[1] Dr. Hafeez Malik (2009), pp.61-63

Iqbal is also reported to have been a frequent visitor at Jinnah's Hampstead residence in 1932, when the latter was living in self-imposed exile and the former was in London for attending the Third Round Table Conference.[1] He is supposed to be among those (along with Liaquat Ali Khan) who urged Jinnah to return home.[2]

In any case, Jinnah was one Muslim leader of British India whose personal magnanimity matched Iqbal's lofty imagination, and the two became inseparable in the popular Muslim imagination after Jinnah's return to India. This had some basis in fact: on the first visit of Jinnah to Javid Manzil in 1936, Iqbal prepared his twelve-year-old son to receive 'a great personality'. When the shy boy displayed hesitation in answering Jinnah's rhetorical question about what he would like to do when grown up, Iqbal remarked that he was waiting for Jinnah to tell him what he should do.[3]

Jinnah included Iqbal at the top of the list while announcing the names of the Central Parliamentary Board of the Muslim League in May 1936.[4] As mentioned earlier, Iqbal also became the president of the provincial branch of the board. He retained that post until a little before his death when he had to relinquish it due to failing health.[5] In the subsequent election, held in 1937, the League lost Punjab to the Unionist Party headed by Sir Sikander Hayat, whom Iqbal didn't trust but with whom Jinnah had to make a pact. Iqbal's timely warning to Jinnah to beware of the new ally probably went a long way to save the League from getting absorbed by the Unionist Party in Punjab.[6]

---

[1] Dr. Hafeez Malik (2009), p.281
[2] Dr. Hafeez Malik (2009), p.281
[3] Dr. Javid Iqbal (Urdu; 2008), p.622
[4] Dr. Hafeez Malik (2009), p.283
[5] Dr. Hafeez Malik (2009), pp.283, 289
[6] Jinnah's foreword in Iqbal (1943/2001), p.8

*What Then Is To Be Done, O Nations of the East? With the
Masnavi 'The Traveller'* (1936)

This was the title of the eighth book of his poetry (in Persian, 'Pas
Cheh Bayed Kerd Aye Aqwam-i-Sharq Maa Masnavi Musafir'). It
was a masnavi. The first part, 'What Then Is To Be Done...', was
self-published from Lahore in October 1936. The second part,
'The Traveller', had already been published in a limited edition
for private circulation in November 1934 but the second edition,
published in 1936, was appended to the eighth book.[1]

The title of the first part, 'What Then Is To Be Done, O
Nations of the East?' was reminiscent of the Russian
publications that had similar titles: the novel by Nikolai
Chernyshevsky, Tolstoy's rejoinder and Lenin's manifesto.

Iqbal's masnavi had been undertaken while he was in
Bhopal for treatment of his chronic illness, and the spirit of Sir
Syed Ahmad Khan appeared in his dream, advising him to ask
the Prophet to pray for his health. Iqbal did that in a Persian
masnavi but preceded it with several chapters, making it a
manifesto of economic, social and political reform for the
nations of the East – a fitting tribute to the memory of Sir Syed.[2]

'You know it very well that monarchy is about the use of
power', Iqbal said to the readers. 'This power, in our times, is
commerce. The shop is now an extension of the throne. They are
collecting profit through commerce, just as governments collect
revenue through taxation'.[3] His advice to the nations of the East
was to build self-esteem by holding fast to their ideals, and by
attaining economic independence. Politics was either a unifying

---

[1] Now included in Iqbal (Persian; 1973), pp.797-882. For publication history,
see Shafique (2006/2007), p.188 and Hashmi (Urdu; 1982/2010), pp.176-179
[2] Iqbal (Persian; 1973), p.844. The prelude, however, begins with Rumi asking
Iqbal to deliver a message, just like the first book, *Secrets and Mysteries*. See
Iqbal (Persian; 1973), pp.803-805
[3] Iqbal (Persian; 1973), p.842

force, 'The Wisdom of Moses'; or it was a divisionary force that enslaved others, 'The Wisdom of Pharaoh'.[1]

A versified travelogue of Afghanistan was an appropriate appendix to a manifesto for the nations of the East because Iqbal believed the buffer state to be the heart of Asia: it had started its evolution into a nation-state under the poet-king Ahmad Shah Abdali in 1747, a decade before British colonialism got its foothold in South Asia.[2]

'Islam and Nationalism' (1938)

'How could Husain Ahmed from Deoband utter such nonsense!' This was the meaning of the second line of a short Persian poem that took the Muslim India by storm in February 1938.[3] Written by Iqbal, it refuted the position taken by Maulana Husain Ahmed Madni, the renowned scholar from Deoband, and other 'nationalist ulema' who were supporting the Congress.

This was the last intellectual battle and the opponent belonged to the school that had opposed Sir Syed long ago.[4] The best thing to come out of it was 'Islam and Nationalism', published in the daily *Ehsaan* on March 9, 1938.[5] In addition to

---

[1] Iqbal (Persian; 1973), pp.808-812

[2] While other Asians learnt democracy, the forgotten lesson of Islam, under European tutelage, Iqbal believed the Afghans to be temperamentally suited to democracy due to 'their deep religious spirit, their complete freedom from distinctions of birth and rank, and the perfect balance with which they have always maintained their religious and national ideals.' See Iqbal (1979/2003), p.316

[3] Now included in Iqbal (Urdu; 1973), p.691 [or Iqbal (Urdu; 1990), p.754]

[4] In the ensuing controversy, Maulana charged Iqbal with ignorance of the Arabic language, although Iqbal had earned gold medal in Arabic as a graduate student, had taught it at London University and his doctorate from Munich was in Arabic philology. Still, the charge was picked up by many enlightened authors, including Annemarie Schimmel (1963/1989), p.37

[5] Included in Iqbal (1977/1995), pp.300-313. Due to the failing health of Iqbal, the paper was drafted according to his brief by Chaudhry Muhammad Husain, the trustee of his estate, and was finalized by the dying author with much pain.

refuting the arguments of the Maulana, Iqbal elucidated two points that have become even more relevant in the present times.

Firstly, that some religious leaders and movements in the world of Islam, while appearing to be orthodox, were in fact as much 'under the spell of Europe' as 'the half-Westernised educated Muslims'.[1] Both suffered from 'spiritual paralyses'.[2]

Secondly, 'in the mind of Maulana Husain Ahmad and others who think like him, the conception of nationalism in a way has the same place which the rejection of the Finality of the Holy Prophet has in the minds of Qadianis' and this would be 'clearly demonstrated only when a Muslim historian gifted with acute insight, compiles a history of Indian Muslims with particular reference to the religious thought of some of their apparently energetic sects'[3].

The Gift of Hijaz (1938)

The ninth, and the last, book of Iqbal's poetry was published from Lahore in November 1938, seven months after the author's death.[4] It comprised of Persian quatrains and Urdu poems. The title was The Gift of Hijaz (Armughan-i-Hijaz).

The Persian quatrains were thematically arranged and included an imaginary travelogue to the tomb of the Prophet. The Urdu section contained mainly poems (and some quatrains), but the masterpiece that eclipsed all other attractions of the

---

[1] Iqbal (1977/1995), p.301
[2] Iqbal (1977/1995), p.312. Hence the likelihood of the 'half-Westernized educated Muslims' and the orthodoxy agreeing on some obscurantist definition of Islam, different from what the masses actually recognize as their religion.
[3] Iqbal (1977/1995), p.313
[4] The Persian section is now included in Iqbal (1973b), pp. 883-1028, and the Urdu section in Iqbal (Urdu; 1973), pp.643-692 [or Iqbal (Urdu; 1990), pp.693-755]. For publication history, see Shafique (2006/2007), p.196 and Hashmi (Urdu; 1982/2010), p.68

volume was the last long poem of the late poet, 'The Devil's Parliament', originally written in 1936.[1]

The Devil had remained an interesting character in Iqbal's poetry at least since 1923. Presented here as a flamboyant and imperious overlord of evil, he was shown consulting his five counsellors on the various possibilities for a new world order to be set up after a second world war that had now become imminent. The counsellors debated the potential threats from various revolutionary and egalitarian ideologies, but the Devil informs his disciples that Islam was the only potent threat to the satanic forces in the long-term. Since the believers were unlikely to be defeated openly, the best strategy was to lure them away from the dynamic aspects of Islam by using religious issues themselves as bait, making the believers so otherworldly that they may never put their mind to the affairs of the world.

Death and immortality

On February 7, 1938, Iqbal dictated what would turn out to be his last Urdu poem (although a few more verses would follow in Persian). An apt ending to his poetic career, the poem was called 'The Human Being'.

Some other verses, composed in Persian around this time, were also going to become very famous as the premonitions of a dying poet who anticipated immortality:

> Will the old song return, or no?
> Will another breeze arrive from the Hijaz, or no?
> The time of this *faqir* has come –
> Will there be another who knows the secret, or no?

> If such a one comes with the knowledge the secret,

---

[1] Iqbal (Urdu; 1973), pp.647-657

Give him songs that would soften the hearts;
For the conscience of nations is purified
Either by a Moses, or by a thinker who plays on the
      flute.[1]

He was pronounced critically ill on the evening of April 20. It was decided that the treatment would be changed the next day but he was not very likely to make it through the night.

His thirteen-year-old son entered the bedroom in the late hours. Unable to see him due to cataract, Iqbal asked who he was. Upon hearing that it was Javid, he made a pun on the name gleefully, 'I would rather that you *become* Javid!' (since the name means 'immortal' or 'eternal' in Persian). He then requested the trustee, Chaudhry Muhammad Husain, to read out 'An Address to Javid' from *Javid Nama* to the boy when he grows up. This was the last time the boy saw him alive.

Sometime before dawn, Iqbal felt congestion in the chest. He asked for the physician, and the attendants advised that it would be better if the physician was not disturbed just yet, since he had stayed up the whole night and had left shortly ago. 'It will be too late otherwise', said the poet-philosopher, and recited the Persian quatrain he had composed a few days earlier: 'The time of this *faqir* has come...'

The attendants rushed to call the physician, but the end came first. Only his servant of long time, Ali Bux, was with him and was holding him. He later said that Iqbal refused to take pain killers because they contained sedatives, and he didn't want to miss the unique experience of dying. He pointed to his chest and said, 'It's here,' and passed away with almost a sigh.

---

[1] Iqbal (Persian; 1973), pp.894-895. Translation of the first four lines has been modified from Mustansir Mir.

Burial

He used to pray that he should not live longer than the Prophet, who had passed away at the age of sixty-three lunar years. He died just a little before reaching that age.

Obituaries and special issues of newspapers began to flood the scene even before he was buried near the main entrance of the Badshahi Mosque, Lahore, on the night of the same day, April 21. His death was widely mourned, especially by the Muslims but also by a large number of fans from other religions – especially Hindus, Sikhs and Christians. Condolence messages, obituaries and reminiscences came out from by celebrities including Gandhi, Tagore, Jinnah, and many more. They were published in local and international press. Much of this material was anthologized in volumes that soon launched the birth of an industry of books, journals and media about Iqbal that thrives to this date, and still expanding.

One thought was commonly expressed by those who knew him personally. It was that the real Iqbal was still living through his writings. This initial feeling, expressed by most of his acquaintances, was going to be corroborated by history in less than a decade from his death.

The Pakistan Movement

Only two years after his death, the annual session of his political party, the All-India Muslim League, was held at a walking distance from his grave and turned out to be the most heavily attended session of the party until that time. A resolution was unanimously adapted to the effect that the Muslims of India would not accept anything less than independent states in the areas where they were in a majority.

The proposed state, which came to be called Pakistan, was believed to be the idea of Iqbal. This was openly acknowledged even by Jinnah, now known as Quaid-e-Azam ('the Great Leader'). He frequently mentioned Iqbal as 'a friend, guide and philosopher',[1] 'our National Poet'[2], 'the philosopher of the National Renaissance of Muslim India'[3] and 'the sage, Philosopher and National poet of Islam'[4]. He also bestowed on Iqbal the greatest tribute that could possibly be paid to a poet:

> If I live to see the ideal of a Muslim State being achieved and I were then offered to make a choice between the works of Iqbal and the rulership of the Muslim state, I would prefer the former.[5]

The election of 1945-46

The last general election commenced in British India in the winter of 1945 and was completed in early 1946. The All-India Muslim League contested it on the basis of a single-point agenda: *Pakistan.*[6] It was the first instance in the history of modern democracy that a people were explicitly asked whether they desired to establish a new state or not, and it was up to them whether a state should come into being or not.

The Muslim League won 100 per cent of the 30 seats allocated to Muslim candidates in the Central Legislative Assembly. In the Provincial Legislative assemblies, it had an overall success rate of 87 per cent, including 89 per cent (75 of 84 Muslim seats) in Punjab, and 94 per cent (112 of 119 Muslim seats) in Bengal, the two most important provinces in view of

---

[1] Condolence message issued by Jinnah on the death of Iqbal, published in *The Star of India,* April 22, 1938.
[2] Message delivered at Iqbal Day in Lahore in 1944; quoted in Rahim (2004), p.xxi
[3] Jinnah's letter, dated August 9, 1941; facsimile reprinted in Razzaqi (1979/2003), unnumbered page after the table of contents.
[4] Jinnah's foreword in Iqbal (1943/2001), p.6
[5] Speech delivered on March 25, 1940; quoted in Rahim (2004), p.xix.
[6] For details, see Karim (2010), p.130-131.

the Pakistan question. This was the verdict that the community of Iqbal – the Indian Muslims – eventually gave on the proposal he had made sixteen years earlier, and the verdict fulfilled the prediction he had made at that time. He had called it 'the final destiny'. If so, it turned out to be not something imposed by Fate, but a destiny through free will and choice. The choice was not different from that which Barkhia had made in the story.

Chronology[1]

The Date of Birth

'I was born on the 3rd of Dhu Q'ad 1294 A.H. (1876 A.D.)', Iqbal wrote in the 'Lebenslauf' of his Ph.D Thesis (Below). Iqbal usually quoted 1876 as the year of his birth approximately but the Islamic date actually corresponded to November 9, 1877 A.D. as pointed out in Rozgar-i-Faqir (Vol. 2) in 1963 and later ratified by two special committees appointed for this purpose by the Bazm-i-Iqbal in late 1972 and the Federal Ministry of Education in 1974. The findings seem to be genuine but they are sometimes subjected to unfounded suspicion since they matched the expedient needs of the Government of Pakistan – India had already celebrated the Iqbal Centenary in 1973!

The mistaken date of birth, February 22, 1873, was first mentioned in the Lahore-based Urdu daily *Inquilab* on May 7, 1938 (sixteen days after Iqbal's death) and it later gained currency through Iqbal's first standard biography written by the editor of the same newspaper in 1955. The entry in the Municipal Register of Sialkot, on which this date was based, is now seen as unrelated to Iqbal. Other suggested dates include December 29, 1873 (suggested in 1971 by a family member), 1875 (mentioned on Iqbal's Middle School Certificate) and December 1876 (miscalculated by Iqbal and his brother from the Islamic date actually corresponding to November 9, 1877).

---

[1] The chronology presented here is taken from Shafique (2006/2007), pp.203-

The Early Years: Up to 1904

15TH CENTURY
Baba Loal Hajj, a Brahmin from the Sapru caste in Kashmir turns Muslims; he was an early ancestor of Iqbal

LATE 18TH OR EARLY 19TH CENTURY
Shiekh Jalaludin, descended from Loal Hajj, migrates to Sialkot with his four sons; among them is Iqbal's grandfather Shiekh Rafique (alias Fiqua)

C. 1837
Iqbal's father Shiekh Nur Muhammad is born as the eleventh son, and the first surviving one, of Shiekh Rafique and his wife Gujri

C. 1857
Shiekh Nur Muhammad is married to Imam Bibi from a Kashmiri family residing in Sambaryal

1859
Atta Muhammad, the first son of Shiekh Nur Muhammad and Imam Bibi is born

1861
hiekh Rafique and his extended family moves to the house that was later to become known as Iqbal Manzil

C. 1865
Shiekh Nur Muhammad makes an aborted attempt at a job with the ACC of Sialkot and afterwards launches his own business in making and selling caps that can be worn by men and women alike

1870
SEPTEMBER 6, Talay Bibi is born to Shiekh Nur Muhammad and Imam Bibi; she is their second daughter (the first daughter was Fatima Bibi, whose date of birth is unknown)

208.

C. 1873

A second son is born to Shiekh Nur Muhammad and Imam Bibi and dies infant; Shiekh Rafique falls victim of cholera epidemic along with his younger son whose family is now supported by Shiekh Nur Muhammad

1877

NOVEMBER 9 (Friday 3 Du Qa'd, 1294 AH), Iqbal is born

C.1879

Infant Iqbal loses the vision of his right eye when leeches are applied as a traditional medical treatment

C. 1880

Atta Muhammad gets married and finds a job with the Civil Works in the army; Iqbal's younger sister Karim Bibi is born

1882

Iqbal attends early education at the mosque school of Maulvi Umar Shah (d.1925)

1883

Iqbal shifts to the mosque school of Maulvi Ghulam Hassan after Umar Shah stops teaching; Iqbal's youngest sister Zainab Bibi is born; family friend and liberal educationist Syed Mir Hasan persuades Shiekh Nur Muhammad to send Iqbal to the Scotch Mission School for modern education

1885

Iqbal passes Grade 1 on 8 APRIL, securing highest marks in the class

1888

Iqbal passes the upper primary examination (5th grade)

1891

Iqbal passes the Third Middle (8th Grade) in FEBRUARY

1893

Iqbal passes matriculation (10th Grade) on the day of his marriage to Karim Bibi, a slightly older girl from a well-to-do Kashmiri family in Gujrat (Punjab); joins Scotch Mission

College; his earliest known poems had started printing in popular magazines by now and he was taking guidance from Dagh Dehlvi through correspondence

1895

Iqbal passes the F.A. Examination (high school, or 12th Grade) in 2nd Division (276 marks out of 570) in APRIL; joins bachelor classes in Government College to study philosophy, English literature and Arabic, and shifts to Lahore (later residing in the college hostel); DECEMBER, receives acclaim in a poetry recital in Bazar-i-Hakeeman (Lahore)

1896

Iqbal's first daughter Meraj Bano is born; Anjuman Kashmiri Musalmanan, a community service organization for and by the Kashmiri Muslims of Lahore is formed in FEBRUARY; Iqbal is a founding member and recites stanzas about Kashmir;

1897

Iqbal secures 2nd Division in B.A., and first position in the subjects of English literature and Arabic (medals and degrees were distributed by the Lieutenant Governor of Punjab the following January)

1898

Thomas Arnold (later Sir) shifts from M.A.O. College (Aligarh) to Government College (Lahore); Iqbal is his only student in M.A. Philosophy; Iqbal must have failed the exam once in his first attempt (unless he didn't appear at all); Iqbal's first son, Aftab, is born on JUNE 23

1898

Appears for obtaining a degree in law in DECEMBER; fails the paper on Jurisprudence when the results are announced next month

1899

Secures 3rd Division and a medal in M.A. (Philosophy) as the only candidate in the subject in APRIL; has already applied for the post of McLeod Arabic Reader at Oriental College, where Thomas Arnold is going to be the acting Principal; Iqbal reports on duty from 5 MAY for a salary of Rs.74/Annas14 per month; as it would turn out, he would serve this institution in intervals: May 1899 to December 1900, July 1901 to September 1902, November 1902 to May 1903; rents a house in the vicinity of Bhati Gate; from JULY he joins the administrative body of Anjuman Himayat-i-Islam, a Muslim community help organization in Lahore with special focus on rehabilitation of widows and orphans

1900

Receives wide recognition for reciting his poem, 'The Orphan's Lament' in the annual session of Anjuman Himayat-e-Islam on FEBRUARY 24; his request for reappearing in the degree for law without attending the classes again is refused on JUNE 21; his first known paper, 'The Concept of Absolute Unity' (completed in MARCH) is printed in *The Indian Antiquary* in SEPTEMBER

1901

Temporarily appointed Asst. Professor in the Philosophy Department of Government College for about a month on JANUARY 4 for a salary of Rs. 200 per month; as it would turn out, he gets the lucrative position again in October 1902 (in the Dept of English) and then from JUNE 1903 till his resignation in late 1908 (at the end of a long leave of absence that started in September 1905); writes an elegy for Queen Victoria; recites 'The Orphan's Address to the Crescent of Eid' in the annual session of Anjuman Himayat-i-Islam in FEBRUARY and temporarily takes up teaching English Literature at Islamia College (a venture of Anjuman Himayat-i-Islam) till JULY; gets wider recognition from the publication of his poem 'The Himalaya' in the first issue of Makhzan, a romantically inclined literary magazine that soon becomes the main outlet for Iqbal's poems in print; around SEPTEMBER he appears for public service examination for the post of Extra Asst. Commissioner and gets rejected on medical grounds (apparently due to his defective right eye)

1902

FEBRUARY, recites some minor poems in the annual session of Anjuman Himayat-i-Islam

1903

Develops affection for the singing girl Ameer Begum, which lasts at least till late next year; 'The Pearl-laden Cloud', recited in the annual session of Anjuman Himayat-i-Islam in MARCH becomes Iqbal's most popular so far (though he would include only one stanza in his anthology *The Call of the Marching Bell* later); Atta Muhammad gets arrested on charges of financial corruption during the summer and Iqbal travels to Quetta to clear him out

1904

Thomas Arnold leaves for England in FEBRUARY, and Iqbal's job at Government College gets permanent the next month with an increment of Rs.50; he recites 'The Picture of Grief' in the annual session of Anjuman Himayat-i-Islam, the first of such poems that would be included in his anthology *The Call of the Marching Bell* many years later; while visiting his brother in Abottabad he delivers a lecture on 'National Life'; soon after his return to Lahore he writes 'The Indian Song' (Saray jahan say achha Hindustan hamara), which receives instant national acclaim; NOVEMBER, his first published book appears in Urdu, *Political Economy* (Ilm-ul-Iqtisad)

The Formative Years: 1905 – 1913

1905

SEPTEMBER 2, Iqbal leaves Lahore for studies abroad; visiting Delhi on the way, he boards a steamer from Bombay and arrives at Dover on 24th; enrols with the Trinity College (Cambridge) on OCTOBER 1 as advanced student of Bachelors and obtains a Matriculation Certificate from the

University on OCTOBER 21; enrols with Lincoln's Inn (London) on NOVEMBER 2 for Bar at Law.

1906

AUGUST–SEPTEMBER, Shiekh (later Sir) Abdul Qadir and Musheer Husain Kidvai visit Istanbul; their first-hand account of Turkey on the eve of modernization may have left a mark on the mind of Iqbal

1907

MARCH 7, *Development of Metaphysics in Persia* submitted as dissertation for Bachelors degree (subsequently granted on JUNE 13); APRIL 1, meets Atiya Fyzee in London; JULY (around 20th), arrives in Germany and stays at Heidelberg to prepare for viva voce on his dissertation submitted at the University of Munich for PhD; meets Emma Wegenast and develops a friendship with her; NOVEMBER (first week), returns to London after obtaining a PhD in Arabic from the University of Munich; temporarily replaces Thomas Arnold as teacher of Arabic during his absence from the School of Oriental and African Studies at London University

1908

Development of Metaphysics in Persia published by Luzac & Co. (London); JANUARY 22, mails his resignation to the post of Asst Professor at Government College (Lahore); FEBRUARY, delivers a lecture on Muslim mysticism at Caxton Hall (London) under auspices of Pan-Islamic Society; MAY, joins the All India Muslim League (London Branch); JULY 1, called to the Bar at Lincoln's Inn; leaves for India on 3rd, and writes a poem on Sicily on his way before arriving in Lahore on 26th; JULY, paper 'Political Thought in Islam' published in *Sociological Review* (London); OCTOBER, applies for practice in the Lahore Chief's Court (permission subsequently granted on 20th) and sets up his office; DECEMBER 27-29, attends the annual session of Mohammedan Educational Conference at Amritsar and joins the delegation of Kashmiri Muslims before Nawab Saleemullah Khan

1909

Resumes active participation in the activities of Anjuman Himayat-i-Islam (Lahore); FEBRUARY 6, elected General Secretary to the newly formed Anjuman Kashmiri Musalmanan; APRIL 10, paper 'Islam as a Moral and Political Ideal' presented at the Annual Session of Anjuman Himayat-i-Islam, Lahore (paper was subsequently published in The Observer, same month); MAY, reluctantly agrees to teach Philosophy at Government College (Lahore) through special arrangement with the Secretary of State (the courts needed to be directed to hear Iqbal's cases after his classes in the morning; Iqbal took charge of classes on OCTOBER 12 and continued till end of the next year); sometime this year, Iqbal also joined the editorial committee of Indian Cases Law Reports, a specialized magazine from Lahore

1910

MARCH 2, nominated Fellow to the University of Punjab; visits Hyderabad (Deccan) on a ten days casual leave from the University (MARCH 18-27); starts writing his notebook Stray Reflections; DECEMBER, farewell lecture on the poetry of Robert Browning delivered at Government College (Lahore); marries Sirdar Begum, but consummation is postponed

1911

MARCH, presents paper 'The Muslim Community – a Sociological Study' at Mohammedan Anglo-Oriental College (Aligarh)

APRIL, 'The Complaint' (Shikwah) recited at the annual session of Anjuman Himayat-i-Islam; DECEMBER, presides over the annual session of the Mohammedan Educational Conference at Delhi where he is also offered garlands by Shibli Nomani on behalf of the Muslims of India

1912

FEBRUARY, poem 'The Candle and the Poet' composed (subsequently recited at the annual session of Anjuman Himayat-i-Islam on 16 APRIL); NOVEMBER 30, recites poem

'An Answer to the Complaint' (Jawab-i-Shikwah) as part of fundraising for the Turks in the Balkan War (1912)

1913

Marries Mukhtar Begum from Jallundhar and the previous marriage to Sirdar Begum is also consummated now; SEPTEMBER 7, visits Cawnpur for a day to see the Commissioner on behalf of protestors arrested for the mosque case; meets Akbar Allahabadi and Hakeem Ajmal Khan on his way back

The Middle Years: 1914-22

1914

Portions of unfinished Persian poem 'Secrets of the Self' (Asrar-i-Khudi) recited at the annual session of Anjuman Himayat-i-Islam (Lahore); NOVEMBER 9, mother Imam Bibi passes away

1915

SEPTEMBER 12, Persian long poem 'Secrets of the Self' (Asrar-i-Khudi) published

OCTOBER 17, Iqbal's daughter Meraj Bano passes away

1916

JULY 8, first recorded complaint of kidney pain in Iqbal's life

1917

JULY 28, Article 'Islam and Mysticism' published in *The New Era*, a periodical from Lucknow (other contributions to the magazine around this time include 'Stray Thoughts', 'Muslim Democracy,' 'Our Prophet's Criticism of Contemporary Arabian Poetry,' 'Touch of Hegelianism in Lisanul 'Asr Akbar,' and 'Nietzsche and Jalaluddin Rumi')

1918

Persian long poem 'Mysteries of Selflessness' (Ramooz-i-Bekhudi) published; JUNE, second edition of 'Secrets of the Self' (Persian) published with major revisions

1919

Appointed Dean, Oriental Faculty at the University of Punjab; DECEMBER 14, elected General Secretary of Anjuman Himayat-i-Islam; same month he attends the joint session of the Khilafat Conference and the All India Muslim League in Amritsar (among other participants were included Hakeem Ajmal Khan, M. K. Gandhi and the Ali Brothers – Iqbal's poem 'Imprisonment' was addressed to the latter)

1920

Secrets of the Self, translation of 'Asrar-i-Khudi' by R. Nicholson is published from McMillan (London)

1921

JUNE–JULY, visits Kashmir for the first time for about a fortnight to plead a case

1922

APRIL 16, recites poem 'The Khizr of the Way,' at the annual session of Anjuman Himayat-i-Islam (Lahore)

The Peak Years: 1922-30

1923

JANUARY 1, Iqbal gets knighted; recites poem 'The Dawn of Islam' at the annual session of Anjuman Himayat-i-Islam (Lahore); MAY 1, Persian anthology *The Message of the East* (Payam-i-Mashriq) published

1924

SEPTEMBER, first Urdu anthology *The Call of the Marching Bell* (Baang-i-Dara) published; OCTOBER 5, younger son Javid born to wife Sirdar Begum; other wife Mukhtar dies in childbirth on 21st; Urdu Course compiled in association with Hakim Ahmed Shuja for lower secondary classes

1925

Presents paper on 'Ijtehad in Islam,' to a gathering at Islamia College; read verses from the Turkish poet Zia Gokalp

1926

DECEMBER 6, gets elected to the Punjab Legislative Assembly

1927

MARCH 10, speaks on education in the Punjab Legislative Assembly; APRIL 16, presents paper 'The Spirit of Muslim Culture' at the annual session of Anjuman Himayat-i-Islam (Lahore); JUNE, Persian anthology *Persian Psalms* (Zuboor-i-Ajam) published; JULY, supports selection on merit to public services in a speech in the Punjab Legislative Assembly; NOVEMBER, joins the Shafi faction, supporting the Simon Commission, against the Jinnah faction of the opposite opinion after split in the All India Muslim League

1928

FEBRUARY 23, opposes the injustices inherent in the existing methods of agricultural taxation while speaking to the Punjab Legislative Council; APRIL 18, presented a paper on the Muslim Philosophy at the annual session of Anjuman Himayat-i-Islam (Lahore); MAY, visits Delhi for medical treatment of kidneys by Hakeem Nabina; DECEMBER 31, leaves for a trip to South India for lecturing on reconstruction of religious thought in Islam

1929

JANUARY 1, attends the All India Muslim Conference in Delhi; till the 19th he is visiting Madras, Bangalore and Hyderabad (Deccan) to deliver three lectures: 'Knowledge and Religious Experience,' 'The Philosophical Test of the Revelations of the Religious Experience,' and 'The Conception of God and the Meaning of Prayer' and also meets the ruling Nizam in Hyderabad (Deccan); APRIL 14, delivers lecture on the necessity of a deeper study of the Quran; article 'A Plea for Deeper Study of the Muslim Scientists' published in Islamic Culture, Hyderabad (Deccan) the same month; MAY, his name is turned down for appointment as justice to the Lahore High Court (former Lahore Chief Court); NOVEMBER 19, delivers a lecture at Aligarh where he is also offered an honorary DLitt

1930

MAY, *Six Lectures on the Reconstruction of Religious Thought in Islam* is published from Lahore; AUGUST, Younger daughter Munira Bano is born; AUGUST 17, father Shiekh Nur Muhammad dies in Sialkot; DECEMBER 29-30, presides over the annual session of the All India Muslim League at Allahabad, suggesting (on the 29th) the amalgamation of the north-western Muslim majority provinces of India for a balance of power in the region as well as a renaissance of Islamic thought

The Later Years: 1931-38

1931

APRIL, Participates in All India Muslim Conference;

MAY 10, participates in the meeting of Muslim leaders of India at Bhopal (called by the ruler of the state Nawab Hamidullah Khan to facilitate consensus on the issue of joint electorate versus separate electorate)

AUGUST 14, Kashmir Day celebrated in Punjab (Iqbal was one of the convenors) to support the protest movement in the valley

SEPTEMBER 8, Leaves for participation in the 2nd Round Table Conference stopping in Delhi (9th) and Bombay (10–12th) on the way;

NOVEMBER 1, 'Minority Pact' formed during the Conference; 16, dissociates himself from the Conference; 18, reception at Cambridge; 20, informs the Secretary of State about his decision to leave the Conference; 21, leaves for Italy where he stays from 22 to 29; 25, meets deposed king of Afghanistan Ameer Amanullah to whom he had dedicated *The Message of the East* (1923); 26, delivers lecture at the Royal Academy, Rome; 27, meets Mussolini;

DECEMBER 1–4, trip to Egypt; 5, arrives in Palestine by train to participate in the Islamic Conference; 6, visits Jerusalem; 5–15 stays in Palestine; 15–17, waits for the ship at Port Saeed; 30, returns to Lahore via Bombay (28) and Delhi (29)

1932

FEBRUARY, *Javid Nama* (Javid Nama), his epic poem in Persian, published

MARCH 6, First Iqbal Day celebrated under auspices of the Islamic Research Institute, Lahore; 21, presides over the All India Muslim Conference (Lahore) and delivers address

JULY 25 Statement on Sikh demands published, asking the Sikh community to see the communal problem in the larger perspective of constitutional progress in India

AUGUST 24, Statement on the Prime Minister's Communal Awards (AUGUST 19) published

OCTOBER 17, Idarah Muarif-i-Islamia established through an announcement (Iqbal is one of the founders); Iqbal leaves for participating in the 3rd Round Table Conference via Bombay (19–22)

NOVEMBER 12, arrives in London; 17, first session of the Conference; 24, reception given by National League (London);

DECEMBER 20, leaves London for Paris; 21, meets Bergson in Paris

1933

JANUARY, arrives in Spain; visits Cordova, Granada, Seville, Madrid and other places; 24, delivers lecture 'Spain and the Intellectual World of Islam' in Madrid University; 26, Returns to Paris

FEBRUARY 10, boards ship for India from Venice; 22, arrives in Bombay; 27, returns to Lahore

MARCH 1, presides over extensive lecture by Ghazi Rauf Pasha, dissident colleague of Ataturk in Jamia Millia College, Delhi

JUNE 20, Resigns from the All India Kashmir Committee

OCTOBER 20–NOVEMBER 3, trip to Afghanistan on invitation from King Nadir Shah of Afghanistan to advise on educational reforms (Sir Ross Masud and Syed Sulieman Nadvi are also invited)

DECEMBER 4, Honorary DLitt offered by the University of Punjab

1934

JANUARY 10, fatal illness starts after eating vermicelli with curd on the Eid Day

MAY, invitation received from Oxford University for Rhodes lecture (Iqbal chooses 'Time and Space in Muslim Thought' as his topic but it is found unsuitable by the University and the lecture could never happen eventually due to his prolonged illness)

JUNE 29, visits Sirhind with son Javid (nearly 10 years old)

JULY 1, becomes president of Anjuman Himayat-i-Islam

NOVEMBER, 'The Traveller' ('Musafir', a versified travelogue of Afghanistan in Persian) published; construction of new residence 'Javid Manzil' starts; 17–25, trip to Aligarh to deliver a lecture

DECEMBER 13, Honorary DLitt conferred by the Muslim University, Aligarh

1935

JANUARY, *Gabriel's Wing* (Baal-i-Gabreil), comprising of his Urdu poems, published; 30, presides over extensive lecture by Halida Adeeb Khanum, dissident colleague of Ataturk at Jamia Millia College, Delhi

JANUARY 31–MARCH 7, trip to Bhopal for electrotherapy in Hamidia Hospital

MARCH 8, consults Hakeem Nabina in Delhi on way back from Bhopal; 10, returns to Lahore

APRIL, construction of Javid Manzil completed

MAY 14, 'Qadianism and Orthodox Muslims' published in The Statesman, Calcutta, as Iqbal's rejoinder to the Governor of Punjab's advice to the Muslims (Iqbal's statement launched a series of arguments); 20, shifts to Javid Manzil; 24, Sirdar Begum dies

JUNE 1, stipend of Rs.500 per month issued by Nawab Hamidullah Khan of Bhopal

JULY 15–AUGUST 28, Second trip to Bhopal for electrotherapy

OCTOBER 25, participates in the Centenary of poet Hali (1835–1914) in Panipat

1936

JANUARY, 'Islam and Ahmadism' published in *Islam*, Lahore, in three instalments, in response to the criticism of Jawaharlal Nehru on Iqbal's previous statement

APRIL, visited by Jinnah at Javid Manzil, Lahore; elected president of the Punjab Muslim League and starts his efforts to organize a provincial Parliamentary Board for the party through which the League could unite the Muslims of the province; 12, recites Urdu poem 'Heavenly Tune' ('Naghma-i-Sarmadi', later renamed 'No God but God' – 'La ilaha il Allah') at the annual session of Anjuman Himayat-i-Islam, which turns out to be his last public performance

MAY, last long poem 'The Devil's Parliament' written in Urdu

JULY, *The Blow of Moses* (Zarb-i-Kaleem), comprising of his Urdu poems, published; 29, Honorary DLitt conferred by Dacca University

OCTOBER, *What Is To Be Done, O Nations of the East?* (Pas Cheh Bayad Kerd, Aye Aqwam-i-Sharq), his last Persian mathnavi published (to which 'The Traveller', published in 1934, is appended some time later)

1937

APRIL, consults again Hakeem Nabina of illness that has turned severe now, affecting eyesight (voice had already fainted away to mere whisper)

DECEMBER 13, Honorary DLitt conferred by Allahabad University

1938

JANUARY 1, New Year message broadcast from All India Radio

MARCH 1, Honorary DLitt conferred by Usmania University, Hyderabad (Deccan)

MARCH 9, 'On Islam and Nationalism' published in *Ehsaan*, Lahore

APRIL 21, Dies in Lahore

NOVEMBER, *The Gift of Hijaz* (Armughan-i-Hijaz), comprising of his Persian and Urdu poems, published posthumously

References

While the following references are likely to satisfy most readers, if you do not find here what you are looking for (or think that a reference is amiss in the text itself), please feel free to send a personal inquiry to marghdeen@gmail.com

With regards to the following, it may be noted that the name of Iqbal appears in several variations on the title pages of his works. It has been standardized here 'Iqbal, Dr. Sir Muhammad', followed by square brackets giving the name as it appeared on the published book, if applicable.

Afzal, Muhammad Rafique (Urdu). *Guftar-i-Iqbal* [The Speeches of Iqbal]. 1969. Lahore: Idara-i-Tehqiqat Pakistan, 1986

Ahmad B.A., Syed Naseer (Urdu). 'Urdu Adab Ki Islami Tehreek'. *Tulu-i-Islam,* Vol.1, No.1, October 1935, pp.32-40. [Edited and published by Syed Nazeer Niazi, Lahore]

Ahmad, Prof. Dr. Riaz. *All India Muslim League and the Creation of Pakistan: A Chronology* (1906-1947). Islamabad: National Institute of Historical and Cultural Research, Centre of Excellence, Quaid-i-Azam University, 2006

Ali, [Dr.] Parveen Shaukat. *The Political Philosophy of Iqbal* (Second Edition). Lahore: Publishers United, 1978

Alvi, Amjad Saleem, ed. (Urdu). *Iqbaliat-i-Mehr.* Lahore: Mehr Sons Pvt. Ltd., 1988

Chaghatai, M. Ikram. *Goethe, Iqbal and the Orient* [Revised]. 1999. Lahore: Iqbal Academy Pakistan, 2003

Cornelius, Justice A.R. (2004) 'Ideological Foundation for Democracy in Islam', inaugural address to the Iqbal Day celebrations, April 21, 1964. In Khawaja Abdur Rahim (Ed.). *Iqbal, the Poet of Tomorrow,* pp.93-107. Lahore: Iqbal Academy, Pakistan

Dar, B.A. (Compiled and Edited by). *Letters of Iqbal.* Lahore: Iqbal Academy Pakistan, 1978

Daram, Dr. Mahmoud; and Marziyeh S. Ghoreishi. *Shakespeare and Nezami.* Lahore: Iqbal Academy Pakistan, 2013

Das, C. R. *Freedom Through Disobedience.* Madras: Arka Publishing House, 1922

Durrani, Saeed Akhtar (Urdu). *Iqbal Europe Mien* [Iqbal in Europe]. Lahore: Iqbal Academy Pakistan, 1985

Durrani, Saeed Akhtar (Urdu). *Navadir-i-Iqbal Europe Mien.* [The Relics of Iqbal in Europe]. Lahore: Iqbal Academy Pakistan, 1995

Faizi, Atiya Begum. 'My Impression of Iqbal'. *Illustrated Weekly of Pakistan,* April 16, 1950, p.31

Hasan, Dr. Riffat. *The Sword and the Sceptre.* Lahore: Iqbal Academy Pakistan, 1977

Hashmi, Dr. Rafiuddin (Urdu). *Tasanif-i-Iqbal ka Tehqiqi-o-Tauzihi Mutalaa* [A Study in Research and Explanation of the Publications of Iqbal]. 1982. Lahore: Iqbal Academy Pakistan, 2010 (Revised and enlarged 'reprint' of the original published in 1982)

Husain, Dr. Sultan Mahmood (Urdu). *Allama Iqbal kay Ustaad Shamsul Ulema Maulvi Syed Mir Hasan* [*The Teacher of Allama Iqbal, Shamsul Ulema Maulvi Syed Mird Hasan*]. Lahore: Iqbal Academy Pakistan, 1981

Iqbal, Dr. Sir Muhammad ['Iqbal M.A., S. M.']. *The Development of Metaphysics in Persia.* London: Luzac & Co., 1908

Iqbal, Dr. Sir Muhammad ['Sir Mohammad Iqbal']. *The Reconstruction of Religious Thought in Islam.* London: Oxford University Press, 1934

Iqbal, Dr. Sir Muhammad. *Stray Reflections, the Private Notebook of Muhammad Iqbal; also includes: 'Stray Thoughts'.* Dr. Javid Iqbal (Ed.). 1961. Lahore: Iqbal Academy Pakistan, 2006

Iqbal, Dr. Sir Muhammad. *Letters and Writings of Iqbal.* B.A. Dar (Ed.). 1967. Lahore: Iqbal Academy Pakistan, 1981

Iqbal, Dr. Sir Muhammad ['Iqbal'] (Urdu). *Kulliyat-i-Iqbal Urdu* [Complete Poetical Works of Iqbal in Urdu]. Lahore: Sheikh Ghulam Ali and Sons, 1973a.

Iqbal, Dr. Sir Muhammad ['Iqbal'] (Persian). *Kulliyat-i-Iqbal Farsi* [Complete Poetical Works of Iqbal in Persian]. Lahore: Sheikh Ghulam Ali and Sons, 1973b.

Iqbal, Dr. Sir Muhammad. *Speeches, Writings and Statements of Iqbal* (Third Edition). Latif Ahmad Sherwani (Ed.). 1977. Lahore: Iqbal Academy Pakistan, 1995

Iqbal, Dr. Sir Muhammad ['Allama Muhammad Iqbal']. *Discourses of Iqbal.* Shahid Husain Razzaqi (Ed.). 1979. Lahore: Iqbal Academy Pakistan, 2003

Iqbal, Dr. Sir Muhammad ['Iqbal'] (Urdu). *Kulliyat-i-Iqbal Urdu* [Complete Poetical Works of Iqbal in Urdu]. Lahore: Iqbal Academy Pakistan, 1990

Iqbal, Dr. Sir Muhammad. *Letters of Iqbal to Jinnah, Foreword by Quaid-e-Azam.* Mohammad Jehangir Alim (Ed.). Faisalabad: Daera Maaref-i-Iqbal, 2001 (Based on work published in 1943)

Iqbal, Dr. Javid (Urdu). *Zindah Rud* [The Living Stream]. Revised Edition. Lahore: Sang-e-Meel Publications, 2008

Kalorvi, Sabir, ed. (Urdu). *Tarikh-i-Tasawwuf.* 1985. Lahore: Maktaba Tameer-i-Insaniyat, 1987

Karim, Saleena. *Secular Jinnah & Pakistan: What the Nation Doesn't Know.* Co. Mayo (Ireland): Checkpoint Press, 2010

Karim, Saleena. *Systems.* Nottingham: Libredux Publishing, 2012

Kamran, Gilani (Urdu). *Iqbal Aur Hamara Ehed* [Iqbal and Our Times]. Lahore: Maktaba-e-Aliya, 1977

Khan, Nawab Sir Zulfiqar Ali. *A Voice from the East.* 1922. Lahore: Iqbal Academy Pakistan, 1982

Laswell, Harold D. and Abraham Kaplan. *Power and Society: A Framework for Political Inquiry.* 1950. New Brunswick: Transaction Publishers, 2013

Laswell, Harold D. *Politics: Who Gets What, When, How.* Whittlesey House: McGraw-Hill book Company, Inc., 1936

Malik, Dr. Fateh Muhammad. *Reconstruction of Muslim Political Thought.* Islamabad: National Book Foundation, 2013

Malik, Dr. Hafeez. *Iqbal in Politics: Adapted from 'Zinda Rood', a Biography of Allama Iqbal by Dr. Javid Iqbal.* Lahore: Sang-e-Meel Publications, 2009

Malik, Dr. Nadeem Shafiq (Compiled and Edited). *The All India Muslim League and Allama Iqbal's Allahabad Address, 1930 (Archives of the Freedom Movement, Volumes No.153 & 154).* Lahore: Iqbal Academy Pakistan, 2013

Malik, Hafeez (Ed.). *Iqbal, Poet-Philosopher of Pakistan.* New York: Columbia University Press, 1971

Malik, Hafeez. 'The Marxist Literary Movement in India and Pakistan'. *The Journal of Asian Studies,* Vol. 26, No. 4, August 1967, pp.649-664. Association for Asian Studies. Retrieved from http://www.jstor.org/stable/2051241 on February 5, 2014

Mango, Andrew. *Atattürk.* 1999. London: John Murray, 2000

Mir, Mustansir. *Iqbal (Academy Edition).* Lahore: Iqbal Academy Pakistan, 2006

Niazi, Syed Nazeer (Urdu). *Iqbal Kay Huzoor.* Lahore: Iqbal Academy Pakistan, 1971

Pirzada, Syed Sharifuddin. *All India Muslim League Centenary Souvenir.* Lahore: Nazaria-i-Pakistan Trust, 2008

Qaiser, Dr. Nazir. *A Critique of Western Psychology and Psychotherapy and Iqbal's Approach.* Lahore: Iqbal Academy Pakistan, 1994

Qaiser, Dr. Nazir. *Creative Dimensions of Iqbal's Thought.* Lahore: Iqbal Academy Pakistan, 2012

Rahim. Khawaja Abdur (Ed.). *Iqbal, the Poet of Tomorrow.* Lahore: Iqbal Academy Pakistan, 2004

Read, Herbert. 'Readers and Writers'. *The New Age.* Vol.29, No.17, pp.200-201. London: The New Age Press Ltd., August 25, 1921

S. K. Mittal and Irfan Habib. 'Towards Independence and Socialist Republic: Naujawan Bharat Sabha'. *Social Scientist* Vol. 8, No.86, September 1979, pp.18-29. Jacob Eapen (Ed.). Trivandrum: Indian School of Social Sciences

Schimmel, Dr. Annemarie. *Gabriel's Wing.* 1963. Lahore: Iqbal Academy Pakistan, 1989

Shafique, Khurram Ali (Urdu). *Iqbal, Darmiani Daur* [Iqbal, the Middle Period]. Lahore: Iqbal Academy Pakistan, 2012

Shafique, Khurram Ali (Urdu). *Iqbal, Ibtidai Daur* [Iqbal, the Early Period]. Lahore: Iqbal Academy Pakistan, 2008

Shafique, Khurram Ali (Urdu). *Iqbal, Tashkeeli Daur* [Iqbal, the Formative Period]. Lahore: Iqbal Academy Pakistan, 2010

Shafique, Khurram Ali (Urdu). *Irtabat-e-Harf-o-Maani.* Lahore: Iqbal Academy Pakistan, 2007c

Shafique, Khurram Ali (Urdu). *Psycho Mansion.* Karachi: Fazlee Sons, 2011a

Shafique, Khurram Ali (Urdu). *Rana Palace.* Karachi: Fazlee Sons, 2011b

Shafique, Khurram Ali. *Iqbal: An Illustrated Biography.* 2006. Lahore: Iqbal Academy Pakistan, 2007

Shafique, Khurram Ali. *Shakespeare According to Iqbal.* Lahore: Iqbal Academy Pakistan, 2010

Shafique, Khurram Ali. *The Beast and the Lion.* Lahore: Iqbal Academy Pakistan, 2007

Shafique, Khurram Ali. *The Republic of Rumi: a Novel of Reality.* 2007. Lahore: Iqbal Academy Pakistan, 2009

Shafique, Khurram Ali. *2017: The Battle for Marghdeen.* Nottingham: Libredux Publishing, 2012

Panipati, Muhammad Ismail (Ed.; Urdu). *Khutbat-i-Sir Syed* [The Lectures of Sir Syed]. 1973-4. Lahore: Majlis Taraqqi-i-Adab, 2009

Panipati, Muhammad Ismail (Ed.; Urdu). *Mazameen-i-Sir Syed, Hissa Panjum* [The Essays of Sir Syed, Volume 5]. 2nd Reprint. Lahore: Majlis Taraqqi-i-Adab, 1990

Spengler, Oswald. *The Decline of the West.* [English translation by Charles Francis Atkinson published in 1926]. New York: Alfred A. Knopf, Inc., 1927

Tolstoy, Leo. *What Must Then We Do?* [Translation by Aylmer Maud published in 'The World's Classic' series in 1925; reprint of a revised edition 1942]. Retrieved from http://vidyaonline.org/dl/whatthenmustwedo.pdf on April 11, 2014

Tanvir, Hina (Tr.). *Javidnama* (abridged). Dr. Sir Muhammad Iqbal. Lahore: Iqbal Academy Pakistan, 2006

Wells, H. G. *Outline of History: Being a Plain History of Life and Mankind.* [Revised and rearranged Third Edition of work originally published in 1920]. New York: The Macmillan Company, 1921

Wolpert, Stanley. *Jinnah of Pakistan.* 1984. Karachi: Oxford University Press, 1989.

Other sources

Eleanor Roosevelt, Speech 'On the Adoption of the Universal Declaration of Human Rights', delivered 9 December 1948 in Paris, France. Retrieved on November 19, 2013, from americanrhetoric.com/speeches/eleanorrooseveltdeclarationhumanrights.htm

http://www.banglapedia.org/HT/B_0412.HTM

Join the Club

We hope that readers will take *Iqbal: His Life and Our Times* as a launching pad for further explorations in Iqbal Studies, especially from the perspective of implementing his ideas. We intend to provided continued support as long as we can, and welcome you to the Marghdeen Learning Centre (MLC), which can be visited (virtually!) at www.marghdeen.com

Many of the sources cited in this volume can be found there directly or are linked to from there.

The MLC also offers online courses in Iqbal Studies, which are certified by Iqbal Academy Pakistan, and provide an in-depth understanding of Iqbal's perspective on history, literature, politics, religion and education. To stay updated, you may also like subscribe to the author's free online newsletter by sending a blank email to therepublicofrumi-subscribe@yahoogroups.com

Any inquiries related to Iqbal Studies can be sent to marghdeen@gmail.com

The Republic of Rumi: a Novel of Reality

By Khurram Ali Shafique

The thread that runs through the poetry of Iqbal and the function of his lectures as an explanation of his poetry had been touched upon in Iqbal Studies briefly, but this was the first attempt to articulate the architectural whole of Iqbal's canon in order to show the intricacy of the design intended by him.

The Republic of Rumi: a Novel of Reality was first published by Iqbal Academy Pakistan in 2007, and was described by Muhammad Suheyl Umar, the director, as 'a narrative that is remarkably readable and accessible without losing the depth that should be expected in such a work. This is a book for our times and of our times.'

It forms a companion volume with *Iqbal: His Life and Our Times*. If you don't find it in a bookstore near you, please feel free to send your inquiry to marghdeen@gmail.com

Iqbal: an Illustrated Biography

By Khurram Ali Shafique

Printed in a coffee-table format, this book has been described as a treasure-trove of information, illustrations and relics about Iqbal as well as being a compelling, easy to read, and frank account of the personal, poetical, intellectual, political and spiritual aspects of his life.

The author received the Presidential Iqbal Award for this work, which was published in English in 2006 and since then has been translated into many languages including German, French, Bosnian, Urdu and Persian.

Readers of *Iqbal: His Life and Our Times* may be particularly interested in this work which contains additional biographical material. If you don't find it in a bookstore near you, please feel free to send your inquiry to marghdeen@gmail.com

The Author

Khurram Ali Shafique is an historian and educationist, and the author of biographies, screenplays and numerous articles in English and Urdu languages. He is the founding director of the Marghdeen Learning Centre, which provides unique online courses on Iqbal's philosophy, and he is also a research consultant at the Iqbal Academy, Pakistan.

Shafique's publications include *2017: The Battle for Marghdeen* (2012), *The Republic of Rumi: A Novel of Reality* (2007), *Samandar Ki Awaz Suno* (Urdu, 1993) and a comprehensive biography of Iqbal in Urdu in six volumes (three of which have been published so far). He wrote the TV movie *Iqbal: An Approach to Pakistan* (2009). His *Iqbal: an Illustrated Biography* (2006) won the Presidential Iqbal Award in 2011, and has since been translated into a number of languages.

At present he is working on a new biography on Cyrus the Great (title forthcoming).

Visit Shafique's websites:

Marghdeen Learning Centre: http://www.marghdeen.com
Republic of Rumi website: http://www.republicofrumi.com

www.ingramcontent.com/pod-product-compliance
Lightning Source LLC
La Vergne TN
LVHW051553080426
835510LV00020B/2970